PRAISE FOR
SILENCE TO STRENGTH

"This collection of stories from Sixties Scoop survivors is
heartfelt, deep, truthful, and positive. Writing personal
stories of early trauma and loss are medicinal: seeing your
story written by you is medicine that leads the way. It takes
courage, perseverance, and support, to stay the journey.
Christine Miskonoodinkwe Smith, a Sixties Scoop survivor
herself, provides space for other survivors to write, and tell
their own stories, for the healing aspect of what this process
accomplishes—'to let out the pain that we hold inside.'
Reading through the veils of colonial silence/violence, to
the strength that propels one onward, I thought of Blood
memory—a kind of genetic memory that flows through
the generations. Asking questions of one's life story leads
to asking many more. These stories of survival all speak of
hope; hope that their stories will reach others silenced by
their past, and give them strength to open the doors to their
own healing journey."

—Atik Bird, author of *The Percy Papers*

T0112992

Writings and Reflections on the Sixties Scoop

SILENCE to STRENGTH

Edited By Christine Miskonoodinkwe Smith

KEGEDONCE PRESS, 2022

Published by Kegedonce Press
11 Park Road, Neyaashiinigmiing, ON N0H 2T0
Administration Office/Book Orders: P.O. Box 517, Owen Sound, ON N4K 5R1
www.kegedonce.com

Printed in Canada by Trico Printing
Art Direction: Kateri Akiwenzie-Damm
Design: Chantal Lalonde Design
Cover art by George Littlechild: "Horse Spirit, Helper, Brother" (2011)

Library and Archives Canada Cataloguing in Publication

Title: Silence to strength : writings and reflections on the Sixties Scoop / edited by Christine
   Miskonoodinkwe Smith.
Names: Smith, Christine Miskonoodinkwe, 1973- editor.
Identifiers: Canadiana 20220421145 | ISBN 9781928120339 (softcover)
Subjects: LCSH: Sixties Scoop, Canada, 1951-ca. 1980. | LCSH: Interracial adoption—Canada. | LCSH:
   Indigenous children—Canada. | LCSH: Adopted children—Canada.
Classification: LCC HV875.7.C2 S55 2022 | DDC 362.734089/97071—dc23

For Customer Service/Orders
Tel 1-800-591-6250 Fax 1-800-591-6251
100 Armstrong Ave., Georgetown, ON L7G 5S4
Email: orders@litdistco.ca

We acknowledge the support of the Canada Council for the Arts which last year
invested $20.1 million in writing and publishing throughout Canada.

Canada Council   Conseil des arts
for the Arts   du Canada

We would like to acknowledge funding support from the Ontario Arts Council,
an agency of the Government of Ontario.

ONTARIO ARTS COUNCIL
CONSEIL DES ARTS DE L'ONTARIO
an Ontario government agency
un organisme du gouvernement de l'Ontario

TABLE OF CONTENTS

INTRODUCTION

Silence to Strength: Writings and Reflections on the Sixties Scoop is a collection of writings by seventeen Sixties Scoop survivors. It details their experiences of adoption, loss of culture and community and how they have chosen to rise above it all.

I learned through my writing that the very act of putting pen to paper was essential to exorcise the pain I felt within and that it was essential to my healing journey. Though writing and its process is different for everyone, I believe it contains a tremendous potential for healing. In part, this is because writing distracts us from our problems, and it is through writing that we learn to cultivate the quality of absorption—becoming deeply immersed in our work and allowing ourselves to let out the pain that we hold inside.

Silence to Strength is a writing platform that I wanted to offer other Sixties Scoop survivors because I wanted to help them see that, through story, we can offer the mainstream public a chance to hear how assimilationist policies have impacted the Indigenous peoples of Canada. I also wanted to be able to assist other survivors in going from silence (keeping our stories inside) to strength (telling our stories), and to show that it is also possible to move forward in our healing.

Lastly, we are telling the Canadian government, "You may have tried to destroy us, but we are here, we have survived, and we are strong."

WORDS

BY TYLER PENNOCK

1

adoption is

a veil
a shape softening
barrier
replacing true things
like touch
warmth
and detail
with space
distance

a scrim
meant for
shadows
and filling
the unknowns
with whatever your
mind can muster
instead
of knowing

a darkness
on
which we
can scratch
our internal
difference

so the light can enter

2

there's a place I carry
that traps love

the way any other
manufactured material might –
        forcing trillions of reflections
        refractions each
        stealing energy
until it can't be perceived

so quick you'd think   silence
              darkness

its undisturbed
natural state

rarely knowing the strength
of things that once disturbed it
or how their atrophy
      leaves warmth
      to be remembered

3

I wish I could talk to the people who conceived this policy movement, to see how they considered its violent nature and decided
that its purpose was reason enough, to know how they grant the
wounds formed of its careless, thrashing intervention –

4

            words
are all I have

print   words
government   words
            other words
            official words
            not-my-words
            printed words
            digitized words
            saved words
            protected words

stuck in a yellow file folder and kept in the back closet words

my mother kept
in a clock drawer:
            inviolable words
            legal words
            weighted words
the holding force
of a singularity

words   binding heft
words   shy of the love
words   the state sent to replace
words   sublimating
love   words

with cracks in them
only a child can notice

5

things a mother saves
for her child
that no one but her hears

6

things a child hopes to hear
in every interaction

that can't

repair

what

was taken.

SHE EMBODIES GRACE

BY TERRY SWAN

Imagine angelic wings holding your blood red-heart as it beats in rhythm with Mother Earth. It floats in an endless expanse of cosmic sky. Tiny particles of darkness rest on the brilliant crimson, shading the areas that have been wounded and require light.

This is the story of Miiskoodeywiin,[1] my heart journey.

~

I remember the exact colours of the blanket on the bed. It was a night sky with red, blue, purple, and golden yellow stars. I can remember when my mom held me under it, I would look at those stars and float, travelling to a far-off place. She said grandma sewed it and I loved cuddling wrapped in layers of love.

Sometimes my mom would read me books, other times she shared stories. I am unsure if the stories were true, but it did not matter. On cold winter nights, she would make us hot chocolate at bedtime. Sometimes, it was so hot that it scalded the inside of my mouth, but I did not care. Just to be with my mom, all snuggled up, warm and cozy, was irreplaceable. It was all I needed.

Through the bedroom window, we would look together at the bright stars outside. The flickering ones, the faraway ones, and the falling ones. She would tell me which ones were our grandmas and grandpas and all our relatives who had died. She said that both of us will go home to that same place.

She would point out the turtle's back, the bear, and all the other animals.

---

1 "Bright Red Heart" in Cree, as given to me by Elder Ma-Nee Chacaby.

My mom was so special. I knew how special she was by the way she looked at me with her deep dark brown eyes. Her eyes spoke volumes. Without words, I felt that she loved me with every ounce of her being.

This is how I imagine my humble beginnings. I have no conscious memory of her.

~

At the age of three, I met a new person I was supposed to call Mom too. I arrived in the car driven by the social worker at the new home. I got out of the car and the social worker got my bag out of the trunk. I remember asking her how long I was supposed to be visiting this person.

See, I was in foster care with a woman who was taking care of my sister and me. This was all a bit confusing.

We walked up to the door and there she was. A very nice woman with a beautiful smile. She was just so friendly. I was a cute little thing. I had really curly hair, and was a little roly-poly, or so my adopted mom told me years later. I looked at her and asked her if she was going to be my mommy and she asked me if I would like that. I said yes and that was when her home became my new home.

This new home was well kept. There were many books on the bookshelf. There seemed to be a place for everything. I was scared that I would mess things up and get in heck for that. The most amazing thing about this home was my bedroom. It was a room I had all for myself! It had a dresser, pictures on the wall, a bed and a short-wave radio! There were clothes on hangers in the closet, and there were dolls, and a most beautiful pink jewellery box.

The most important and valuable thing to me was that radio. I slept with the radio every night. It was my comfort. I loved listening to music, searching for talk shows from around the world, hearing people's voices that helped soothe my anxiety by transporting me to a faraway place. It was a little bulky, holding it with me under the blankets, but the radio was mine. It was my lifeline and kept me company, while I lay waiting for my real mom to come and get me and bring me home.

She never came.

~

If I were to go back in history, I imagine I would find that my mom, Caroline Theresa Swan, carried soul wounds,[2] shadows of unresolved grief and despair. She was so young, so fragile, with no support, both her parents dying of tuberculosis when she was just four years old. She had no lifeline to help guide her through her trials and tribulations. And without this, she succumbed to taking her own life. She is an angel now always flying above me whispering love notes. She embodies grace in my heart.

In life, my birth mom was a petite woman, standing a mere five feet, two inches. I have in my possession only one picture. I can see a resemblance between us in the sides of her lips as they curl down in contemplation, sometimes in indignation. It can make us both look stern. In comparison to my other relatives in the picture, she is dressed to the hilt for the sombre occasion of the funeral. The other relatives look out of place, but then again perhaps she is. Her knee length high-heeled boots tightly zipped up on the side of her calves, the coat from that generation's fashions with the faux fur. Her hair well-coiffed, all done up in a bun. She is standing there with her hands in her pockets, her shoulders up in the air, perhaps resolute. I see her eyes in mine, the deep dark pools that have many stories to share, her high cheekbones, and the carriage of a face that shows us her resounding spirit. I am my mother's daughter.

I too have many stories to tell. It is hard to know where to start. The story of falling off the little red bike with the big fat tires is a good one. How my neighbour picked me up off the street, blood gushing from my forehead. How my adopted mom would tell me years later as an adult that the reason she did not take me to get stitches was because she thought social services may come and take me away. I still have the scar. I could tell you about the time when I was twelve and I used to go on long walks by myself. One day while living in southern France, I was drawn to the seaside to sing my heart out as the waves crashed on the rocks, as though calling to someone lost in the waves, or hearing my name called from the sea. I have since often wondered if I was guided by a power greater than me in that moment.

I was so independent growing up, a real fireball, a risk-taker. At times it seemed I was scared of nothing. Other times, I was immobilized in terror, protecting a closed heart.

---

2   This concept is detailed in *Healing the Soul Wound* by Dr. Eduardo Duran.

You see, my heart plays an important role in all these stories. I have learned that it encompasses all. There is no greater purpose in life than the role of this living and breathing organ and intelligence. Without it there is no tale to tell, no chronicle of events that can be conveyed without the mentioning of its role and relationship to all of Creation.

~

I am flying high above a lake shaped like a five-pointed star, Achakos[3]. From high above, I see wall tents with stovepipes sticking out of the canvas and further back in the bush are four teepees set up in a circle. I smell the wood smoke coming out of the dwellings.

I love that in dreamtime your senses can be activated, and you experience them as vividly as in waking life.

I see children scurrying around playing and laughing. I see women and caribou hides strewn over poles with dried meat hanging. I smell the loveliness of a rabbit stew cooking as it wafts up to that faculty through the ethers.

I now see a plane land in that tiny cove. I experience uneasiness and one of the four winds blows swiftly and knocks me slightly back, a pang felt in my belly.

Four men and one woman, all moniyaw,[4] get out of the plane. I see them approach the happy encampment and then like a flurry, I see women grab their children and run them into the bush. They are crouched down. I am terrified as I watch from above. I pee my pants. I hear screaming from the children and wailing from their mothers. No men, I see no men. I watch tiny dots of children being coerced onto the plane and it departs. And then like a candle being blown out, echoing silence fills the space. I feel the warm sensation of peeing a bit more. One by one, I see the mothers come out of the bush with their children. I hear shrill cries, I see the fires burning out, then total darkness and I awake.

I remember community members telling us stories similar to those I had dreamed during my travels over the years. They talked about how their grandparents would move further back into the bush so they would never be scooped.

This dream was so close to the feeling of my own apprehension by the Department of Public Welfare, as it was named, in Edmonton, Alberta in 1962. There is no terror greater than that

---

3 "Star" in Cree, *Alberta Elders' Cree Dictionary.*
4 "A White Person" in Cree, *Alberta Elders' Cree Dictionary.*

when a child loses its mother, and the mother loses her child.
A haunting memory forever etched in my unconscious.

It was hard to know how to navigate life after such an injury to my spirit. I left my adopted home when I was sixteen, and never went back.

When I was twenty-five, a life-altering event happened. I woke up from an evening of intense drinking. My drinking career was well established. On Saturdays, I would meet my friends at the bar downtown at noon and stay until last call. Saturdays were the best days because they would bring in the biggest blues artists like John Lee Hooker, Koko Taylor and Long John Baldry. Those were the days and man, could we dance up a storm! That is how I grew to love the blues. I was a seasoned beer drinker. I had already decided that hard liquor got me into way too much trouble.

When I woke up that morning, I had thrown up nineteen times the night before, or so I was told. I have no memory. I now know that all those blackouts at the end of my drinking career were alcohol poisoning. I remember I woke up sicker than a dog, full of a remorse that was so familiar to me. I always had to be with others, because I could not bear the shame alone and I was convinced I was going to die if I kept this up.

My normal became very dark that morning. All those years, I used firewater as a superpower to escape this reality. I believed I was in control, indestructible and infallible. It gave me the illusion that I could fly to the moon, I could conquer any mountain, and most importantly, no one could ever hurt me again.

That morning my will to live just came coursing through my mind so strong, like a breath. I did not want to die. The story unfolds from there: I checked myself into detox and I have remained sober ever since. The incredible will to live was given to me in a brief second that has allowed me to share my story with you today. The will to heal, and to let the life force of the universe come closer, a heart opening, and the beginning of a journey to validate my undeniable faith in something far greater than me.

Over sixty years of life stories fold around me. As my grandmother whispers, intuition strengthens. As I stand at the centre of the universe I am brought back to the teachings of great mystery, the beginnings of all Creation, from the ocean floor, island buried, one million warm bodies sleeping. When I arrive, I know this place called home lives and dwells deep in my heart. Dream buried treasure.

~

I had a mere few years of sobriety when I received the phone call.

I was sitting in my office on a break when the phone rang. I had never heard his voice, and yet I knew it right away. The sound of him, rising out of the vapours, validated my whole existence. I knew in that moment who I was—the blood in my veins, the colour of my skin, my voice and lifeline. His words: "You even sound like my dear late sister, your mother." Resounding. The sound of his voice, returning an echo that I had listened for and never found, until then.

I went home after speaking to him for the first time, remembering his words, feeling them as a part of me already, a part that was always there and yet also missing—simply a profound awakening and remembering of my birthright.

His sister, my mother. My uncle, his niece.

Wearing a brilliant purple turtleneck that night, I looked in the mirror and said out loud, "Yes, you really are an Indian." My voice sounded different. All those years with no validation. My voice missing its echo, no distant hills to bounce and return from to make meaning.

Uncle Tom, you will never ever know what it meant to me, the day you travelled all those miles to confirm, not just with words but with the voice that spoke them, that you were my uncle, and I was your niece.

~

Ceremony.

When my birth mom passed in 1973, our traditional ways for taking care of her spirit had been forgotten. Over the years, I began to understand the significance of our releasing ceremonies. Sometimes our Loved Ones require some help. These ceremonies help the spirit that has not yet crossed over to find peace. I knew that after forty-two years, my birth mom's spirit needed to go home. What a beautiful honouring we did that day. I prepared what I thought might be her favourite foods to feed to her after the ceremony. In a fraction of a human second, she crossed. I saw the Ancestors dancing with joy, dressed in their finest regalia, to the heartbeat of Mother Earth. I rejoiced in oneness with her sacred spirit and voice. From that day forward, I felt her embodiment of grace.

"What I want you to know, my daughter, is that I am safe and very, very happy. I want you to know I'm so proud of who you are becoming. I want you to know you have important work ahead of you. I know that because you are a strong dreamer. You have special gifts. Please remember to teach the children about death and not to be afraid of it. Life does not end. It's so beautiful here, crystal clear and no shadows. You are now carrying on a legacy of hope. I'm always watching over you. You have to learn to ask for help. You must be clear in your intentions. You were born of the generation that is referred to as the quickening time of rapid change. You and all the other like-minded souls cannot wait and sit around any longer. Your people are starving for the teachings of the yellow shawl. The yellow shawl that I wish I could wrap around all of humanity. It brings the spirit of hope. I want you to know I see the strong warrior woman you are and have become. Please stay strong my daughter. Carry on in legacy of my life."

~

And so, at each change of season, I travel deep below the Earth. Cascades of water and obsidian crystals are at her core. I float down on the longest cord and when I arrive, the fires are lit, and they all come in and we celebrate. Life. The timeline and realms blend together. I am a shape shifter. Today, I explode in fiery lava. Another timeline collapsed. I am moving towards infinite possibility.

My name is Keeper of the Stars Woman and I am from the Fish Clan.

RECOLLECTIONS OF A SIXTIES SCOOP SURVIVOR

BY DOREEN PARENTEAU

My name is Doreen, and I am originally from Treaty 4. I grew up and currently reside in Treaty 6. I am married to my husband of ten years and a mother to a three-, a seven- and a nine-year-old. I would like to share my story in hopes that my experience can give other survivors hope and strength and to educate other people about the lasting impacts of Canadian history that has not only affected First Nations peoples, but a history that I am also just learning about as a First Nations woman.

Sharing my story also serves as a healing tool for me. It helps me to be able to acknowledge and understand the trauma, the identity and cultural loss that I have endured by getting it out on paper and out of my head. Even though it was so many years ago it wasn't up until recently (2020) that I have been strong enough to start to learn and heal from it.

I have very few memories and pictures of my biological family and growing up on the Cowessess and Pasqua First Nation reservations where my family was from. I pretty much have no memories of my late mom, who due to terrible circumstances and beyond her strength at the time abandoned me with a family friend who also could not keep and look after me. It was at this time that my time in care, aka "the system"—Child and Family Services— began.

My memories of being in care from a young age bring up many mixed emotions. In the grand scheme of things, once I was finally placed with my forever legal guardian family, my life there with them was pretty good compared to some who were in care. I went into care alone but was miraculously reunited with my younger sister who went into care separately and a short time after me. After spending a couple years moving from short-term foster home to foster home, I remember spending the summer of 1991 at Lac St. Anne summer camp. This was supposed to be an interim fix while they found us a place to go, I wasn't sure of what happened to the family that we had come from or why we couldn't return there but we didn't.

I thought the camp was supposed to be a week-long situation, but I wasn't sure as I had never been to camp before. It turns out that we were there for the duration of the summer months. I remember finally getting news from our social worker that they had a home for us, with an older couple whose kids were already grown up and didn't live at home anymore. I remember as we left the camp and on the drive with our social worker to our new home, a fear came over me; were we going to fit in, were they going to take care of us and like us enough to let us stay?

Although scared, I was hopeful because we had no other options as nine- and six-year-old children. We had to trust that these adults were making choices with our best interest at hand. I hoped that we didn't have to return to that camp we had been at before and that this time things would work out differently. Fear and specifically anxiety are still emotions that I struggle with every day. I have a hard time entering into a situation where I don't know exactly what is going to happen, I hate the feeling of not being in control in certain situations and not knowing what the outcome is going to be. I am an over-planner because if I don't plan things out as much as I can, I worry. Fear and anxiety of "what if?" typically with a negative ending, are strong and hard to control at times.

On August 29, 1991, we arrived at our new foster home. We had a great experience, and we still call these people 'family' to this day thirty years later. The people who took us in were two caring Caucasian people. They were happy to have us regardless of where we had come from or what the colour of our skin was and what we were going through.

It was a nice, clean, safe place to live, even though we did not know how long that would be for. The house was situated on farmland with lots of outdoor space. At the time, I thought we were brave if we spent any time outside. I say brave, because having been in similar situations a few times before, we weren't totally comfortable venturing out of sight on our own in our new surroundings.

Within a few short days of arriving, we started at a new school that was thirty minutes away in the closest town. As we started learning our surroundings, meeting new kids, teachers, and routines, we became familiar with everything whether we wanted to or not. I knew that learning new surroundings wasn't something all the kids around us had to do. In the back of my mind, I felt that some of them had it so good that they probably didn't even realize it. I felt that they had no worries or fears because their everyday routines and surroundings never had to change, and lastly, they didn't have to adapt to as many changes, like my sister and me.

A saying comes to mind: "sink or swim" I felt like we were forced to swim sometimes even if we didn't know how, but the good thing about being a kid when I look back at it now, and after having my own kids, is that I have learned that kids are resilient, and they can adapt quickly.

As we settled into our foster home, our foster mom enrolled us in extracurricular activities. We participated in Ukrainian dance, Girl Guides, and school sports teams that were aimed to help us achieve a sense of belonging and community. We also attended church and Sunday school which taught us spirituality. We learned about growing food because our foster dad grew a large garden that supplied us with a lot of vegetables. We learned about animals and caring for them and my sister even got a few horses of her own to ride and care for.

My foster parents did the best they could as non-Indigenous people bringing up Native children; they enrolled us in Cree class in elementary school where we learned to make some culturally specific crafts and we also learned some basic Cree words. I remember the class having very few kids in it. It wasn't a mandatory class, but an option. Mostly Native students attended. I remember enjoying the culture-specific teachings that were being taught but also at the time, being a kid in care, I also felt I had to stay focused on things like being glad to have a safe place to live, food on the table and a roof over my head. I was also just happy to kind of fit in with the other kids in school who had great life stories. These were the main things my sister and I had concerns about back then. It wasn't so much about our culture, a culture where we had experienced some scary places and people.

We questioned why we would want to learn about "that culture" from people who inflicted so much harm and trauma on us. I am now learning, as an adult, that what happened to us back then was not by any means culture-induced trauma, it was far from it. We did have some contact with some biological family while in care—with my sister's dad's family (we did not have the same dad). They came out to Alberta to visit us a few times from Saskatchewan. We also went with our social worker to Saskatchewan to visit.

There was some fear associated with coming in contact with some of my family because I recall, it wasn't always good times and good memories being with them. It was also never my mom; it was my stepdad and his family. There was a time while in care that these family members tried to get us to come back and live with them in Saskatchewan. I had a lot of apprehension about this possibly happening. I didn't feel like these family members had our best interest at heart, as they had not shown me this previously. They hadn't stepped in to take care of me when I initially went into care, and that was something I always wondered about and questioned for several years while in care.

Maybe my family did culturally have our best interest at heart but security wise, I felt safer and secure when I was at this foster home with this non-Indigenous couple that had taken us in. During our short time there, they had shown me the security, care and love that made me feel I was never in harm's way. There was even a time when our foster family proposed to adopt us and I recall due to Child Services and government protocols, they were not allowed to.

I remember an Indigenous counsellor being brought to our school to talk to my sister and I individually to discuss the possibilities of our care, and to see if he could make a judgment call based on each of our conversations, where the best places for us to stay would be. This was pretty heavy stuff for a kid in Junior High. It's not like there wasn't enough for kids this age to deal with on top of being questioned or pressured by adults in authority to make a choice about where we wanted to live or where we felt safest.

I guess looking back now, if I had known the identity and cultural crisis I would find myself in later, I may have chosen the Indigenous family who offered culture and connection to my sisters' family; technically not mine. However, at that age based on the situation and memories that were ingrained in our minds, things like safety, care and love were ranking higher than the identity and cultural loss at the time.

I have no regrets about the upbringing we chose back then. I feel like if I had chosen back then to lean towards going back to Saskatchewan with that family, I may not be where I am today. My foster family taught me the same life lessons I needed to be a functioning and contributing person to society, minus the Indigenous identity and culture.

My sister and my foster family were only allowed to be appointed as our legal guardians until we were the age of eighteen. We gladly took that deal; I remember having to sign papers for that situation and that was a relief because it meant a few things for sure; signing the papers meant we knew we were going to be in the same place for an extended duration of time, we wouldn't have to worry about whether there was going to be enough food to eat and clothes to wear, and for the most part things would stay the same. I was thankful for that.

I also became grateful that I met a supportive and caring husband, because with thanks to my foster dad, I learned about care and respect and what it looked like. I didn't get the concept of respect of men towards woman from my Indigenous family. I have memories of men being abusive to my mother in drunken states and I have vague memories of checking into women's shelters with my mom.

I remember in my college days going out and partying and going home with boys at the end of the night showing no respect or care for myself because at the time I didn't understand how degrading that was. I just remember one day thinking, "Wow; if I keep this up, I'm going to be like my mom." It was the concept of "many kids from different dads," that scared me from the disrespectful situations I put myself in.

As a mother to three kids now, I do everything I can to provide them with the best childhood that I can give them. I want them to have minimal worries, unlike how I grew up. I learned many lessons from my own upbringing. One of the lessons was that no kid should have to experience "adult issues" and carry them on their shoulders. They need to just enjoy being a child. This was something I didn't have as a child; I had heavy adult decisions to think about and deal with and I didn't really get to just be a kid.

Security and safety vs identity and culture? As a kid in care, those were the questions I always struggled with. Questions like: Are there enough reliable, safe, Indigenous foster families out there? Is the lack of reliable foster homes due to a broken system? Is it due to colonialism? What options do kids in care have?

Lastly, I always wondered if there was any correct answer to these questions that kept circling in my mind In 2019, the Sixties Scoop Settlement and its issues came to light. It was my sister who encouraged me to apply. I was on the fence about all of it, because technically I believed I had the best upbringing I could have; I was one of the lucky ones and that it didn't really apply to me because I felt that I had had a good life.

I didn't really read a lot about the settlement or research it. I had mixed emotions because I was a registered Native, but also looked Caucasian with dark features. I knew that I was treated differently in society than probably most Indigenous people because I didn't look Indigenous.

However, my nationality was usually the first thing people would ask me about. Though I was able to blend in with the majority and found it easier when comments towards Indigenous people came up, there was shame that ran deep inside of me. It was due to my upbringing and childhood trauma that I felt I didn't want to be associated with Indigenous people and I preferred to not be one of them. I believed those rude stereotypical comments I had always heard.

Therein lies an inner conflict to apply as a Sixties Scoop applicant. I applied just before the deadline and was not 100 percent sure what made me apply, but I did. I didn't need the money from the payout as, from the outside eye looking in, I was set up in life. I work, my husband works, we have a house, a car and are able to provide for our family. Regardless of all this, I applied. I didn't even know if I would be accepted as I didn't have a horrible story, like so many have.

When I received the letter of notification that yes in fact my claim was accepted, it was then that I remember thinking to myself,

"Wow." I think it actually rattled me; because I asked myself, "How does this apply to me?"

I had it good because I was so happy with where I was in life. Yes it was rough at the beginning, but I turned out Ok and life was better than it had been. I put the letter away with mixed emotions and I was like, "We will see what happens" and, "I'm not going to let a part of the past that I've buried in the bottom of my soul creep back up and disturb the things that I had worked so hard for."

2020 started rough, because it was right around the time that the pandemic started. I found myself in a triggering traumatic situation that was very similar to what I had experienced in childhood. It brought up the issues of abandonment I had experienced and was also related to substance abuse and mental health. This time though, the roles were changed; I was the person trying to help. I was taking care of an extra child, and experiencing growing concern for this child's parent was difficult. I had to be calm for this child and keep things as normal as possible for them while they were separated from their mother.

I had impending doubt and wonder that made me question the world and the things that had been coming my way which included the initial payment of the Sixties Scoop Settlement. Old feelings resurfaced. I began to feel so much anger and disappointment with the situation around me, and once again questions arose within me and around me about my people, my identity and my culture.

I remember asking myself, "Why is this happening to me? This included thinking back to my mom abandoning me. Many other questions resurfaced such as "What did I do wrong to deserve such disrespect?" "How come my mom didn't want me?" "How come my mom didn't fight harder?" "Why wasn't she stronger?" "How could she do this to me, someone she gave birth to and supposedly loved?"

Those are just some of the questions that I have been able to keep quiet over the years and stuff down. These questions came back to me and got loud once more. I remember a conversation about my current situation in life and how it compared to so many other Indigenous individuals. I asked, "Why would the government give us money?" and "What was that supposed to fix? How was that money going to fix the damage or bring back my identity as an Indigenous person or my culture?"

The individual I was speaking to responded with "Well that's all they can offer is money." It was after that conversation that it hit me, "Wow it's not about the money, it's about educating myself as to why they had to give us the money. I came to the realization that, just as I had to do when I was a young child, I had to find a way to learn, educate and understand who I was and where I came from.

I remember following Shayla Stonechild on social media and being in awe of her owning her Indigenous spirituality and culture and her empowering words from a podcast and thinking to myself, "Wow there's strong empowering proud Indigenous women out there?

I recall Shayla recommending some books. *Sacred Instructions* was the first one; but because it was in audiobook format, I listened to it. I had so many 'ah ha' and 'yes' moments listening to that book. Things started to finally make sense and I started thinking outside my usual trauma response and began learning about residential schools. This is where I learned about my mom attending residential school.

On Orange Shirt Day, I remember posting a picture of my three children and I wearing orange shirts in support of residential school survivors. Even though I had made sure they wore orange on that day in previous years it had way more meaning this year and I took extra effort to explain to them the reason and representation behind the wearing of orange shirts. I shared my story with them about not really getting to know my mom or having her be a part of my life and the reasons why.

When I made that social media post it was like my way to proclaim to everyone that maybe media or even I didn't know my whole story, but I was going to put in the effort to learn more about what had happened, so that my kids didn't have to grow up with questions about their identity, culture and where they came from.

I was doing everything I could for my children because I never received that from my mom, but I kept thinking that they were going to run into the same problem and uneasiness that I had run into and felt for the majority of my life; I was a registered Indian but had not known what that meant or really fully knew who I was or what it meant to be Indigenous.

I know I didn't want my children to have all those questions or have these struggles down the road. It was then that I committed myself to helping them learn more about themselves. It seemed daunting, considering we were in the middle of a pandemic, but I have and continue to do it.

So here I sit in 2021, continuing to be inspired by Indigenous people online representing our cultures and bringing to the forefront the intergenerational traumas of the past that are continuing to affect so many Indigenous people. The second book I read was "*21 Things You May Not Know about the Indian Act*," and that was an eye-opener for me; it shifted my perspective on Indigenous people including myself and my mom and I realized the many things we have had to overcome and still are dealing with and must continue to overcome.

It's interesting how education is empowering but I wish I had known some of this earlier on in my life. But I understand and have learned that the Creator only presents to you what you are ready and able to handle or deal with.

For me, it is my belief that I was ready to acknowledge the pain and trauma from my past and start my healing journey. I've been told it's ongoing with Indigenous people, that we must always be learning to adapt and be open to the healing process. I've learned so much about trauma including what it is and how to move forward positively.

I have heard so many inspiring stories and talks about what we can do as Indigenous people to find ourselves and begin our healing process and I have learned we are in control and it's up to us and how we use our time to heal. Sometimes, I still feel the feelings of doubt or guilt creeping up within, but I didn't realize until I started researching and reading things online about the Sixties Scoop that I had suffered identity and culture loss.

What the government did to so many Indigenous people throughout history, beginning with the residential schools, the Indian Act, and the Sixties Scoop, is unacceptable; the compensation is an act of reconciliation, but the real reconciliation is in truth, education, equality and understanding.

There is a lot from my life as a Sixties Scoop survivor that I can't get back and that the government can't provide but everyone can put in the work to learn their truth and educate themselves, understand the trauma and be open to acknowledging and healing from the past. It is also everyone's responsibility, including those who may not be survivors. There is so much more to these stories than just a government reconciliation payment.

I have not been able to fully reunite with my biological family. I did not know my dad and unfortunately my mom passed before I knew better or was able to reconnect. I have been in contact with my mom's sister, just via Facebook messenger. She has been helpful in telling me things about my mom and her side of the family. I hope in the future to be able to reconnect in person and visit my mother's reserve in Saskatchewan when the time is right for me. I want to continue to learn, educate others and be a voice for other Indigenous people. I know it's not going to be easy, but I feel and know our stories need to be told truthfully and the more people know, the better.

Lastly, though it shouldn't have to be our job to educate others, if we don't, who will? I kept my Sixties Scoop Payment quiet last year and barely told anyone because I wasn't sure how to process it all, but I understand now that it is a good conversation starter, an opportunity to share my story, and bring awareness to the Sixties Scoop which so many people don't even know about or understand the hurt that lies behind it.

SURVIVING

BY ANNA CROXEN

My name is Anna Croxen, and this story is about my life's journey and what survival means to me. It is also describing what life is like for a mixed-breed child in Canada. I am a half black and half Native woman. I was born in 1957, in Halifax, Nova Scotia.

I was born to a young black woman who struggled with depression, great sadness, overwhelming pain and grief. My father was a Mi'kmaq man born in Truro Nova Scotia, but he became very ill after my mom became pregnant with me. He was placed in a hospital for people suffering from tuberculosis, but he passed away in that horrible place. It was not long after he died that my mom was alone and also homeless. She was unable to care for herself, so she surrendered herself over to an unwed mother's home. This home was a place where young unmarried women could live until their babies were born.

When my mother went into labour, she was sent to the nearest hospital to give birth. It was there that she was visited by social workers from the province. The Social Services Department had been continuously involved in my mom's life, monitoring her case closely, which continued shortly after she arrived at the unwed mother's facility. It was part of their protocol. She was told by those social workers over and over again that the best thing for her to do after having her baby was to give it up for adoption. They reminded her that she had no way of taking care of a baby by herself. They also told her that giving her baby up meant that she could start her life over again with a clean slate.

My mother was very vulnerable, lonely and confused, so she believed that they were right. Shortly after my premature birth she left me behind in the hospital. I was born two months early and was underweight. It was required that I stay in the hospital until I was of normal birth weight. I stayed in the hospital for two months before I gained enough weight to be released to the Social Services Department.

It was after my mother left the hospital that she quietly found enough money to move away. I never saw her again during my childhood. It became the hospital and social services workers responsibility to take care of my wellbeing.

Before my mother left, she told a few people what she had gone through and relayed that I was in the care of social services at the hospital. Due to her telling other people about this, a member of my father's family went to the hospital and claimed me as part of their family. This was so the Social Services Department would know I had family before they could legally put me up for adoption.

After a brief investigation, the family was able to provide enough evidence that they were kin folks and the Social Services Department handed me over to this family. I lived with this family for two long years, until the mother of that family began to lose her eyesight and couldn't manage to care for me anymore.

I was returned to the care of the Children's Aid Society. When word got out again that I was back in the custody of Children's Aid, a family member that had raised my mother, who had also been an adopted child, came to look for me.

The adoption disclosure report indicated all the information I share here. Within the same disclosure report, it was also indicated that I was never legally adopted by the City of Halifax's Social Services Department. It read that I was adopted but stated that a family member came and took me home, and this was because they could prove they were blood related. Apparently, that was how things worked back in those days, but that wasn't what I had grown up knowing or understanding. After leaving the first family that took me in, I went to live with a family in a small town, who owned a farm in Nova Scotia.

They taught me how to farm, how to work hard and how to earn my keep. I didn't mind the hard work. I made friends with the animals, fed them and cleaned the chicken coop and barn. Living on a farm was a good experience for me. The woman who took care of me at the farm was very strict, but was also a very kind lady and very nice to me. I remember her telling me stories while she braided my hair, showing me the right way to pick strawberries and blueberries, and showing me that we never took all the berries, because we had to leave just enough for the snakes and other animals. We often picked berries together then we would bake delicious berry pies.

It was her husband that I didn't like very much. He was the opposite of her, and this soon showed in how he treated me. It wasn't long after I moved into their home that he began picking me up on his knee, bouncing me around and feeding me candy with one hand while touching me inappropriately with the other. Though I was only three years old at the time, I remember these things happening to me and it stuck in my mind. I remember it feeling kind of weird, but I thought he was allowed to do this because he was my father. This was very confusing for me, but I never said anything to anyone. I was a child, I got used to it and I enjoyed the candy. But as time went on, it became more invasive.

He would tell me I was a very good girl for keeping our little secret and would buy me gifts for keeping the awful secret—the sexual abuse. Keeping the secret meant I could buy a new dolly or anything I liked. I really liked the gifts just like I liked the candy and so I did whatever he said. He had me programmed from the age of three until it suddenly stopped one day when I was nine years old. He had suffered a heart attack and passed away in the hospital. I never forgot that night, because though everyone else was crying, I think it was the happiest night of my childhood.

I was very quiet because I thought I had prayed him dead. I was scared and happy at the same time, and I got out of going to his funeral by faking sick. Instead, I stayed home in my room and thought that now that he's gone, the pain would stop. What I didn't realize was that years of that kind of abuse plays havoc on your young mind. I had become very damaged from all of his abuse. My little body began craving that kind of touch from boys. I was always trying to fulfill my craving for that touch. I had been programmed for years and was now living with the aftereffects of those years of being sexually assaulted.

I became promiscuous at a very young age, and this led me down a very dark road. At the young age of thirteen, I actually ran away from home. This happened after my middle school track and field teacher attempted to rape me. I didn't want to be with this teacher, so I fought him off. He was an ugly old man, and very mean. He told me if I told anyone what he tried to do to me that he would kill me and that no one would care.

Sadly, I believed him and thought I had better run far away from him before he really hurt me or my family. I was a very young run-away and the streets were a very scary place. The streets were also a very lonely place, but I learned how to survive out there. I probably lived out on the streets for about six months, sleeping from place to place, and panhandling and hustling for money in order to get food and shelter. One night I meant this older boy that hung out with us street kids, but he lived in his family's basement apartment. We became friends and eventually he invited me to his place. I would go to his house, smoke weed, drink beer, and sometimes fall asleep on his couch.

One night while sleeping on his couch I woke up with him on top of me. He took what he wanted and went back to his bed leaving me alone on his couch to cry myself to sleep. He would let me sleep over whenever I wanted to as long as I allowed him to have sex with me. After a few weeks of doing this, he told me he was leaving that he would be moving to Toronto where there was work waiting for him.

A couple of weeks after that he left. I began to feel sick, horribly sick. I went to a walk-in clinic and found out I was pregnant. I didn't know what I was supposed to do. The doctor at the clinic told me that I had choices, and that I didn't have to go through with the pregnancy. I knew that wasn't what I wanted to do, so somehow, I pulled my fifteen-year-old self together and made my way to Toronto to find my baby's father.

It wasn't long after arriving in Toronto that I found him and realized that he had fallen in love with another woman. He wanted nothing to do with me or his baby. He denied ever touching me, called me horrible names and told me to get lost, that he never loved me and that he never wanted to see me again. I left with my head spinning in circles. A few days after that I returned to Nova Scotia.

Upon my return to Nova Scotia, I went back to the little farm where I had previously lived. The lady who had taken me in before welcomed me with open arms and cared for me until I had my baby. I fell in love with this woman, and she became like a mom to me. I cared for her for many years after that, and often visited her with my children. She was ninety-five years old when she passed. I felt fortunate that I was able to love her for so many years and cherish all that she had done for me.

BECOMING A MOTHER AT SIXTEEN

Now that I was a mother, I promised myself that I would be the best mother ever, and that I would do everything I could to love and cherish my beautiful daughter. I was very young and because of my age when I went to the hospital to have my baby the Children's Aid was on my case. They offered to help me. They helped me to get assistance, secure a small apartment, get furniture, and secure the cost of setting up utilities.

I thought I was doing well being a mom. I kept my home clean; I cooked and fed my baby well. She was my best friend. I sang to her because she loved music. I adored her and took good care of her. One day I ran out of diapers and asked my neighbour, who was also my friend, if she could look after my daughter while I went to town to get more diapers. While I was gone the Children's Aid Service Department workers came for a home visit. It was the 70s after all; this was something that the Children's Aid had to do.

My baby daughter was apprehended. It happened after they knocked on my door and not only couldn't find me but thought that my neighbour's brother was taking care of my baby instead of my neighbour. Despite pleas by my neighbour, they scooped my daughter. I came home to my neighbour crying, and though she was trying to explain to me what had happened, I couldn't comprehend the logic behind the Children's Aid's actions. They had left a card with a name address and a number, but when I called, no one answered.

I wanted my baby back! I soon learned that the building that held my baby was like a prison. It was a large brick building with locked doors and had no windows from what I could see. I recall being outside of the building and screaming so loud for my baby, that someone called the police to report that I was making a ruckus. When the police arrived, they told me I was disturbing the peace and that I needed to go home and call them in the morning. I couldn't believe what I was hearing. I didn't want to leave my baby in that place. I continued to bang on the door harder and harder until I couldn't feel my hands anymore. I kept screaming.

Eventually though, I was dragged away by four big police officers and taken to jail. I was charged with disturbing the peace, not to mention that as the police dragged me away, I had kicked and punched the officers, and they wanted to lay even more charges against me.

Those charges impacted my case when it came to getting my baby back. I was refused any visitation with my daughter because officials said I was unstable, and this could cause harm to my daughter. I fought long and hard to get my daughter back, but there were many hurdles that I had to jump over. I felt that my lawyer was useless. I had no family support, no job, no education, no home and most of all no hope. I lost my home because financial support was cut off after my baby was taken. I couldn't pay my rent, so I headed back to the old farmhouse I had grown up in. I felt broken and ashamed.

I fought for a year to get my daughter back, but I didn't have any success. I couldn't beat the system; they had scooped my daughter and I wasn't getting her back. Finally, I gave up the fight and my precious baby was placed in foster care. It felt truly inhumane and cruel that from the day my baby was taken, I wasn't allowed to see her.

BROKEN AND LOST

I decided I couldn't live in a town that stole my child because everywhere I went, I knew I would be reminded of her little face. After getting enough money together to take the train to Toronto, I headed there, thinking I was leaving my past behind me. I wasn't sure why I wanted or decided on Toronto, but I knew my mother lived there somewhere and thought that maybe I could find her. Upon arrival in Toronto, I stayed in a women's shelter, and I went to welfare for assistance They gave me just enough money for me to buy beer and pay for a room.

I didn't really care about anything else. I felt extremely lost and worthless. I was destroyed from the inside out and deeply depressed. I realized I hadn't left my horrible past behind me. In fact, I was still holding on to it. I hardly ate, I drank way too much alcohol and did lots of drugs. I didn't really care what happened to me. I didn't care what drugs I was taking as long as I could get high and forget my life. Sometimes I'd wake up in unfamiliar places and drag my body up from the streets and find my way home to the dump of where I lived. I remember waking up in doorways, on parks benches and in stranger's beds. Then one day I did it. I took too much of something and I ended up overdosing.

I was saved by the ambulance paramedic, and I ended up in a hospital in the mental ward. That was where I met an angel in the form of a woman who took the time to hear my stories and helped me begin the long hard journey towards healing. This woman was very kind, caring, understanding and compassionate. She helped me get set up with intake workers and workers within the community. The programs I was enrolled in really worked for me. It was a new beginning to my life. It wasn't easy, but I really did want to do better for myself, so I continued with what I had to do in order to put my broken life back together. I had survived and knew that I needed to keep on living.

This meant enrolling back into school, finding a part-time job, finding a home, and learning to manage not only my money but also my rehabilitation from drugs and alcohol. It wasn't easy but I was determined to live a better life. After coming so close to death, I really learned to appreciate the new life I was building. I made it through the first year, the second year, and the third year. I graduated and went on to college. I found a good job. Things were going well; I not only found my mother, but we became friends. I met a man, had another child and went onto have three more children.

Before, I had never found true love with any man. That was one thing I couldn't understand. Relationships were difficult, and I never trusted men. I couldn't work through a relationship without my past haunting me. Even with therapy, I somehow always managed to sabotage every relationship I had and would end up alone. I didn't believe I really liked men very much, and I never really cared for a relationship if my babies were there; I had my job and my independence.

For a while, I worked two jobs. I strived for success in everything I did, but it eventually caught up with me. Sadly I, worked myself so hard that I became very ill. I underwent several big surgeries and having to focus on my recovery meant that I was forced to slow down my life. But I survived it all.

MY NEW REALITY

It was in 2015 that I moved to downtown Toronto and realized that I needed to somehow make new downtown connections and build a new community around myself and my kids. I began looking around and came across an Indigenous organization that grabbed my curiosity. I had been thinking about my father and I thought maybe I could find out more about his history, his ancestry, and his heritage. I wanted to learn a little about the other side of me. So, I dropped into the centre for a visit to check out their programs. After walking through those doors, I was intrigued. It was one of the best things I had ever done for myself. I loved the place, and I loved the people, I found my true sense of self there. I attended many things at this organization. This not only included healing circles, but I learned to smudge, pray to the Creator, and I learned about and began to practice the Seven Grandfather Teachings— Wisdom, Love, Respect, Bravery, Humility, Honesty and Truth.

I learned how to drum, bead, make regalia, dance traditionally at Powwows, how to make bannock and also eat and cook wild meat and salmon. All of these things combined helped me to become a whole person again. It helped me see the missing link in my life, and I learned that I needed to know the whole me in order to become one with myself. I am now a healthy and happy senior elder that sits beside other like-minded people that have gone through similar obstacles in their lives, just like I have.

I have sat with Sixties Scoop survivors and residential school survivors. I enjoy the company I keep. I have now been in a happy relationship with a man for eight years now. We are engaged and will be married in 2022. I have a loving relationship with my mother, with my eldest daughter whom I found through my healing journey, who is healthy and happy, and I have a great relationship with my other four children and my eight beautiful grandchildren. I have true friendships that will last till the end of my life. I am a grandmother, a storyteller, a writer, and I am a caregiver to my beautiful mother. I am now happy, and instead of regrets, I now feel I have purpose.

Though my healing journey is ongoing, I feel that I have found my place, I have found my peace, I will never stop doing good things for my spirit. I will continue the good work I do for others. I can now say I love life, and if I can survive all that I have been through, I can say it is possible for anyone out there to do the same. You can change your destiny, change your life and make it a better place to live. All you need to do is find the light. The world needs your story.

Miigwetch

♥

RAINY DAYS

BY MELISSA THOMAS (SIGVALDASON)

There were many rainy days growing up as an Indigenous adoptee. On these types of gloomy days, maybe I would be asked a weird question by a well-meaning stranger or maybe it was in school when we had to discuss our heritage. It was on these days where I felt different and felt like I was an outsider. I would feel bad about being adopted. About not knowing my family or where they were. But these days gave me time to reflect and think quietly about my life. Many thoughts would go through my head.

I would think about my biological parents and about how they didn't want me. I felt like there was something missing from my life, and I felt like something was wrong with me. I focused too often on what happened to me and at times, it really made me feel like I didn't belong anywhere. Now I want to share the story about the life that I was given and what I did to overcome those hard rainy days.

My life began as a baby in Child Family Services. My birth mother lived in a foster care home at the young age of fifteen. My birth mother tried to make things work while taking care of me, but she wasn't able to. She gave me up for adoption. I had one picture of her that was included in my adoption records. It was the day she said goodbye to me.

Her eyes were puffy and red from crying, but she looked like me with her big round face and she had the same long fingers and large hands as me. That was the last picture of her holding me on her lap. She died in her forties before I ever got to see her again.

My birth mother had substance abuse struggles. I often wish that I had been able to see her, even just once. There is little information about how she died and where she went after she left me. The most devastating part is not getting to know my birth mother. Can you imagine never seeing your mother and trying to comprehend how many moments were missed?

I was eventually adopted into a welcoming and loving family. I grew up on a big farm and I have lots of memories of playing outside. I had a horse and lots of dogs and cats. There was even a huge creek to play in each day. My adopted parents loved me as if I was their biological child. I was the youngest of two older siblings. My adopted family is of Icelandic and Ukrainian/German descent. My sister and brother were good to me and treated me well as I grew up. I went to school in a predominantly white community with little to no exposure to my cultural background. I belonged to the community but still felt like I stood out compared to everyone else.

Then every once and while, I had sad days where I would reflect on being adopted. Sometimes the reflections began as a trickle and then turn into a thunderstorm. I badly wanted to fit in with my friends and my family and I often wished I was white. I would tell people I was Metis because that was listed on my adoption papers but deep down, I knew I was a full-blooded Native. I always looked at my adoption papers with my mom and I would talk about them with her. I would always cry because I was so angry at my birth mother for giving me up for adoption without even a letter to say goodbye. It took me a long time to see that she was just a child herself and to come to terms with the grief I was feeling.

I remember telling my adoptive mom that when I was older and rich, I would buy white skin for myself. I was so dark when I was little and even though people didn't exactly say I was different, I just knew that I looked and acted different than most people around me.

When I was in Kindergarten, I came home crying from school one day because a girl said she didn't want to sit by me because I was a "dirty Indian." I didn't understand how I could change that about myself and wished I was the same as everyone else.

I always had an Icelandic last name, and it became a ritual opening for people to ask me, "What's the story behind your Icelandic last name?" They would ask me because I was deep brown in skin colour. I always said, "Oh, I'm adopted" then they would laugh and say, "Oh okay, now that makes sense."

Knowing I was adopted and being questioned about it really hurt my feelings and embarrassed me because it always happened in front of strangers. I didn't get a chance to tell my story in my terms. We, as a society, try to see everyone in tiny boxes that require checking off to understand them.

Another challenging part of being adopted was having no biological ties to my adopted family. I didn't have the same nose or their smaller frame. My adopted family had similar taste in food, or they would all be good at one thing, like baseball. They would always be talking about what it meant to be Icelandic or German/Ukrainian. They would include me in their cultural teachings or jokes because they viewed me as their biological child, but I wasn't in the same category. It was confusing to me because it made me question who I was, what I liked and did not like.

I equated rainy days with my sadness and confusion when people would come and ask me what my mom did for work or when Father's Day came up. I knew I had two moms and two dads. I didn't want to explain it or even explore it, so I just pushed it down and kept on going with my adopted parents being my primary focus.

When I became older and felt like I didn't fit in or when things weren't working out for me, I would pray and talk to my birth mother. I would say, "Why did you do this to me? Why wasn't I good enough? How could you be so cold-hearted leaving a baby alone forever?" I would end up crying myself to sleep. I remember my adoptive parents telling me that I was their child, and I was meant to be with them. They would always say that they chose me, and I was special because they chose me out of all the other children in the world. On those days, my parents would cheer me up enough that I would be able to go on with my life.

When I came to the city to go to university, I was seventeen and naïve when it came to things like riding a bus or buying groceries. I lived with my best friend (who was my older cousin) and she had helped me get by around the city. I truly don't know how I would've gotten through my life without her love and guidance. She is someone that will always be on my side. I eventually became comfortable working and living in the city on my own.

It was during my experience in university that I noticed I was different compared to most students. I felt like they were more fortunate than me and it often made me feel like I was not good enough. I would experience racism in class when everyone would turn to me for answers during the one or two classes where we talked about Indigenous education or when they would say demeaning things about Indigenous people.

The other soon-to-be teachers would ask me for support for lesson plans and it was challenging to be called upon when I was just learning about Indigenous education myself. I felt that I had lost the Indigenous education connection that I would have received from my birth parents, or at least someone in my biological family or at school. I overcame this loss by attending different classes on Indigenous ceremonies, ribbon skirt making workshops, beading moccasins, and birch bark biting. I have been lucky enough to know some Elders that have included me in sweats and Sun Dance ceremonies.

After some time, I went on to receive four degrees from university. I have a Master of Education degree, a post-baccalaureate degree, an Education degree, and a Bachelor of Arts Degree. I never received any funding for school because I wasn't a status Indian. My adoptive parents supported me in my schooling. I am proud of myself for finishing my degrees because I worked so hard, but I have also felt like I let down my ancestors. I did not want them to look down at me for not living a traditional Native life.

I decided to become a teacher. I wanted to become a teacher because I want kids to get all the opportunities in life. Currently, I am teaching Kindergarten and have been teaching for twelve years. I've taught many young brown faces like mine once was. I feel at ease being with them as I know that they are all my relations. It seems like this generation of kids are taught more about Indigenous education and what our traditional ways of being are. It brings me peace and comfort knowing that things like residential schools, treaties, MMIWG and the Sixties Scoop are being discussed in school. It's important for us to learn from our history.

Eventually it was through having my own children that also helped me. Having children of my own and seeing myself in them was nothing short of amazing. They are smart and are proud of who they are, what they look like and often tell people that they are Native. I talk to them about my story, and I talk about Indigenous knowledge and stories. I want them to never go to bed crying and wishing they were different. They will always be loved in the same way I was, but they will not carry the huge burden I faced with being adopted, with people that didn't look like me and didn't know their culture.

It is my hope that by sharing my story, it will help others realize that even though there are rainy days, there will always be something good just around the corner. We learn from the hard days, and they shape us into the people we were meant to be. Remember, there is always a rainbow after the storm.

Melissa Thomas (Sigvaldason) – Rainbow Woman

COULD YOU
"GET OVER IT"?

BY ALICE MCKAY, B.A., B. ED.

In loving memory of my brother, Wilfred John McKay, whose school experience was neither just nor effective and whose death is a grim reminder that some lives still matter more than others; to my family, who are proof of the damage to which oppressed people are susceptible to, but more importantly, are a true testament of strength, courage, and resiliency; and to the good people at the University of Winnipeg Education Centre (WEC), who set me on a path of healing, instilled in me a sense of belonging, and gave me back my power, my voice and my dignity so I could, in the words of Phil Baker, confront the "thornier issues in [my] life."

I lost my nisîmis. Wilfred—or as I called him, Willy—was the youngest child of both nimâmâ and nipâpâ. I was—am—their second youngest child. I will not compare my grief to the grief of our older siblings. What I will say is that I lost something they did not. Before nisîmis's death, I was someone's big sister. By no means was I a good big sister—I was the worst big sister. I abandoned him at a time when he needed me the most. Before abandoning him altogether, I treated him with the utmost contempt. I could never admit it, until now, but I resented him. Why did he get to live with okâwîmâw? To experience okâwîmâw's unconditional love and acceptance? To seek comfort and safety in okâwîmâw's arms? To nestle in beside okâwîmâw when he had a bad dream? The last

43

time the social workers came for us, I was just two years old—I was nimâmâ's pêpîsis, her pêpîsis tânis. Nimâmâ had locked me and nistes out of the apartment and attempted suicide.

When I finally saw nimâmâ again, I was six—it was my birthday. It was the first time I met nisîmis—nimâmâ's new pêpîsis. That was also the day she told me that nipâpâ was murdered— again, I was six. Nipâpâ was murdered when I was four, but all I could think about was nimâmâ's new pêpîsis—how come he did not have to leave, and I did? From that moment, I believed everything they had ever told me—nimâmâ did not love me anymore; did not want me anymore. In my six-year-old mind, she had replaced me, just like they said she would. In that moment, I felt something that I had never experienced before—hatred. Never again did I yearn for nimâmâ, cry for nimâmâ, or think of nimâmâ the way I did before. Until my dying day, long after my spirit leaves this body, I will forever carry the shame and guilt of never having told nisîmis that I love him; never having honoured my sacred role. Why do I get to live, while he does not?

My always forgiving, accepting and loving brothers—I am sorry. I only thought of my own pain and judged you on yours. But this is what *they* did to us. This is what *they* did to my family. *They* say that 'time heals everything' and that we should just get over it. Who even are *they*? Politicians? Social workers? Therapists? Teachers? Middle-aged white men and their jealous wives? *They* are the ones who portrayed us as barbaric savages and then doled out barbaric savagery in the form of policies and legislation that made our genocide and the cruelty *they* continue to exercise against us acceptable. *They* are the people who, quite literally, hand-delivered us to predators, who then robbed us of what innocence we had left, and taught us to lie, and feel ashamed of the things that *they* did.

They are the ones who pitted us against each other to ensure their dirty secrets would remain untold—like their deeply perverse sexual attraction to, and unquenchable thirst for little, brown-skinned boys and girls. *They* are the ones who, in a fit of jealous rage and hatred, called us disgusting and dirty, and then let those men touch us with the same hands that *they* used to steal our innocence, as though *they* were clean. *They* are the ones who inflicted on our mothers and fathers the very cruelty *they* subjected us to, and then taught us to hate and blame our parents for the things *they*, not our parents, did to us. *They* are the ones who poisoned our minds and indoctrinated us with their Eurocentric and racist ideology and reminded us daily of our inferiority. *They* are the people who labelled us as troubled children who are destructive, angry and lie, and did nothing to protect us or help us heal from the things *they* did to us that caused us to be troubled.

They are the people who taught us to suppress the trauma *they* inflicted on us, and gave us poison to numb our pain, and then hurled racist and hate-filled slurs at us. *They* are the ones, in their glass houses with closets jam-packed with the skeletons of dead Indigenous children, mothers and fathers, who demand we 'get over it'—who refuse to acknowledge that our suffering and the violence perpetuated against us did not stop when the last residential school closed.

They are the reason that I could never allow myself to be vulnerable enough to put into words the effects that I feel every single day because of the trauma *they* violently inflicted on me and the damage I struggle to heal from—the trauma and damage that began with my grandparents nearly 100 years ago and is continually perpetuated through the systemic injustices that killed my father and brother. Our stories and experiences are proof of the damage to which oppressed people are susceptible to.

WASPS

BY CATHY PHANNENHOUR

Lately, a memory has been flooding my awareness as I take committed ownership of healing the traumas of a lifetime. It is this: I am submerged in water, eyes wide open, and I see the fear in my dad's eyes. A large, black swarm of wasps has been disturbed and I am under attack. I am five years old. To be stung dozens of times could prove fatal. My father is keenly aware of this.

This is the memory that keeps guiding me as I dive more deeply into trauma therapy. I have been trying to come to terms with being stolen from my parents through the "wisdom" of the Children's Aid Society in 1971. I was a "Scoop Baby," stolen immediately after birth from my young Indigenous mother. I had blocked the agony of those wasp stings for many years, wondering why NOW is this story surfacing. Awareness is guiding me to know that my story is not finished, yet.

When I feel great pain, I reach out to wise women for guidance and support. It was a dear friend and sage who asked me to investigate the Spirit message brought by the wasp. Guided to Colette Baron-Reid, I was stunned to read the following: "Oracle Message—Not all that Spirit creates in nature is easy to love, but when we look through the eyes of the Wasp Spirit, we recognize that even though, sometimes, life stings, there is purpose for pain."[5] I felt resonance. What struck me so deeply was the remembrance of the message my adoptive mother shared with me like a mantra,

---

5   Colette Baron-Reid, n.d. "Wasp Spirit." https://www.colettebaronreid.com/oracle/wasp-spirit/ Accessed June 2022.

many times over the years, that I was unlovable and difficult to love. That included a clear message she gave my former husband, she would advise people in my life to leave me because I was not worth it.

This is the year of my fiftieth birthday. It also would have marked my ten-year wedding anniversary. The anniversary will not be celebrated as we have faced insurmountable challenges. We have decided to go our separate ways, and the pain is deep. The catalyst, or perhaps the final straw, was a recent accident that caused my husband a brain injury and brought with it an awareness of an illness he had been trying to hide. Our worlds changed quickly and irrevocably. In ways I never expected, nor really wanted, the wasp came back.

In her study of Wasp spirit, Baron-Reid goes on to say, "The sting of life may hurt, and you may feel deeply disappointed or even resentful that Wasp Spirit has shown up, but you will soon come to see that Spirit has something wonderful in store for you. You may well come to realize that being stung led to something far better than you had envisioned for yourself."[6] Perhaps, behind the scenes, Wasp Spirit is conspiring with Spirit to ensure that I can grow something of value to me; that Spirit has a plan, and the Wasp is playing its part as a messenger.

Life speaks, doesn't it? Spirit communicates with us in a myriad of ways if we just get quiet enough to listen. I have often looked back with gladness and appreciation that Creator did not answer some of the prayers I sent out. I realize now that Creator always gives me exactly what I need, and more. Today's sting may hurt but something better awaits.

The memory of the near fatal wasp stings as a child has served as a powerful guide. My dad and I spent our summers camped along the shore of the Ottawa River. We enjoyed hours playing in the water, and people often joked of my love for the river. Kicking and screaming, I more often than not had to be pulled in from the water at the end of a glorious day, covered in goose bumps and sporting blue lips. I was happy.

My dad always spent a lot of time with me, playing games such as timing how long I could hold my breath under the water. He taught me to read his lips while I was under water and then jump

6 Colette Baron-Reid, n.d. "Wasp Spirit." https://www.colettebaronreid.com/oracle/wasp-spirit/ Accessed June 2022.

up and guess what he had said. It was usually a message like, "I love you"; "You are so beautiful"; "You are my favourite little girl"; "You mean the world to me"; "Are you tired of the water, yet?" The summer the wasps came was the summer I became very good at holding my breath under the water. Little did I know how much we were preparing to save my life, because it was to the water my father took me and held me under to save me from the wasp attack.

With my father, I was encouraged to play and laugh and run barefoot. On the day of the attack I was running barefoot behind a group of children. It was me who unwittingly found the wasp nest when I ran directly through it and disturbed their nest. The swarm awakened as I stood with both feet planted firmly in their territory. I began to scream. The swarm surrounded me, determined to lash out. I ran towards my father and he guided me to the water, away from what I saw as the safety of his arms. I knew, though, that it was good to go to the river as I loved it and I could hold my breath under its surface for a long time. I loved and trusted my father and that water. I trusted them both with my life. That long run from the woods to beach seemed endless, but I saw my dad starting to run with me towards the water as the swarm kept coming. Our running merged and dad grabbed me by the arm and threw me under the water, holding me down as he took the wrath of the wasp stings. I could see people around my father and I trying to help get that black swarm away from us. As I had been taught, I looked to my father's lips as he sent me comforting messages under that saving river water that it was going to be okay and that he loved me.

I woke up in the hospital that day to a large white light. I needed to be soothed as the pain was excruciating. A beautiful nurse kept telling me it was going to be okay as she scraped the skin on my legs with a lifesaving silver tool. I fell back to sleep and awoke at home hours later to legs that were so swollen they looked like I imagined they would be as an adult. When I look at my fifty-year-old legs today, I am reminded of that time.

I was stung seventy-eight times that summer's day. One hundred would have proved fatal for my height and weight. Even though my dad had to hold me under that water to save my life, I knew I trusted him. He was the only person I could rely on. He was the only one who could have helped me survive that attack. I don't know if I could have trusted anyone else enough to listen. The preparation through innocent summer play saved me. I had someone I could count on. And that has not usually been the case in my life. I have gone on to face much worse and darker trauma in the years following that summer. I may not always understand why my dad felt we had to practice such strange games in the water that year, but he must have been guided by something he could not explain. The wasps came with a message that there is a bigger plan, but it has taken me many years to understand it. My life was being saved in many ways. The message was clear.

As a Sixties Scoop survivor I have come to know I am here for a reason. All of us are. We are part white and part red and both enrich our experience. We may not understand what happened to us or why, but we have the power of individual and collective voice to share a message of hope and healing of trauma for ourselves, our ancestors and for the generation that are birthed forward through us. We bridge a gap between two worlds to bring compassion and awareness through our stories. Those wasps did not kill me, nor did the multiple traumas I have faced. I have become stronger, more resilient and compassionate with myself and with others. I recognize and honour my huge loving heart and extend its goodness to the world. I have a huge respect for wasps and an awareness of their powerful sting. They almost took my life, but I kept standing. I am still standing; a proud, beautiful woman who delights in life. I am an Indigenous woman wanting to make her ancestors proud, and to offer up thanks to Creator for a greater plan that is much better than I can even imagine.

THE MAD CHRONICLES
OF A SIXTIES SCOOP
SURVIVOR

BY LISA WILDER

My name is Lisa, I was born in Winnipeg, Manitoba in 1969, and put up for adoption at birth. I was raised in a Jewish home with two brothers who were also adopted (not Indigenous to my knowledge), by two parents who loved us more than anything in the world. In fact, being adopted was not only never hidden, but it was also part of the reason I knew how much I was loved…. "Out of all the children in the world, we picked you."

I no longer believe in luck; in fact, I no longer really believe in bad or good. What I do believe in are blessings and lessons, both of which you can find in almost any situation. It is only when we find our lessons within the bad, that we can begin to heal enough to create that good.

Sometimes I wonder if being so loved may have added to some of the confusion I felt growing up. I know that must sound crazy to the many survivors out there who would have killed for that love, and by no means am I putting myself in the same category, but just hear me out. On top of never feeling like I quite fit into the community I grew up in (which is putting it mildly), I thought there was something seriously wrong with me because I felt this way DESPITE this love. Then feelings of guilt and shame would set in, bringing along their good friend worthlessness.

When I was thirteen years old, I was allowed access to some general information surrounding my adoption. I remember how excited I was when that day came, I was finally going to access a little piece of "who I was." Along with that excitement, however, was the guilt about wanting and needing that information. If I loved my *parents*, which I very much did, why would this be so important to me? In this way, perhaps I really did fit into the Jewish community—I was living in perpetual guilt.

Guilt and shame, like fear, have no place. They are there only to manipulate your energy to bring on more of those similar feelings, and deter that energy from the important things, like trying to understand who you are. Why do I believe in spirits when nobody else around me does? Why does the sound of a beating drum seem to take me into a trance? Why do I get so much comfort from watching flames of a candle or fire? Why do I feel our earth is alive and has feeling? Why do I feel purified when waving my hand through smoke? Why do I see the interconnectivity of all so clearly? These were not things I learnt through my upbringing, nor did the answers come in that adoption file.

My adoptive parents had already told me that the reason I was placed for adoption was because my biological father was killed in a car accident when my biological mother was pregnant with me. I "knew" this, but there it was in black and white. There was also a very brief description of each.

I am of Metis ancestry on my biological mother's side. Her father was Metis, and her mother Mennonite. There was nothing about my Indigenous blood in my file. When I was in my early twenties, I put my name in the Post Adoption Registry. There was a pull to know more. It was scratching away at me, and then there was the need for a medical history on top of this—never being able to give the doctor an answer when asked if there's any family history of something—adding to the itch. And that is truly what it was like…a continual itch that would never go away.

When I was twenty-six, I got a call from a social worker at the Jewish Child and Family Service. My biological mother had also registered in the Post Adoption Registry and wanted to find me. There was some confusion. She was looking for a boy, not a girl. She had given birth to a girl but was told by the hospital that the baby was going to die and signed what she thought was the authorization for them to take care of my burial.

In order to take care of herself during the latter part of her pregnancy with me, and put a roof over her head, she had to put her one-and-a-half-year-old son into temporary foster care, a decision I myself have often wondered if I would have been strong enough to make. And although she maintained each and every visit she was allowed, while Linda (my birth mother) was in the hospital giving birth to me, my biological brother was being shuffled around foster homes until he was finally sent to Victoria, where he was adopted illegally, and without our mother's consent. It was by the age of seventeen, that my biological mother had lost two children.

The initial period of correspondence and connection with my birth mom was brief. I was already going through a lot in my personal life (again, a major understatement), and through Linda, I learned that the Cinderella story that I had believed around my adoption, was not the real story. In learning about all of this, I never fully understood all the caution I was hearing from my parents and the adoption agency about what you may find out and how it may affect you.

The most important thing for me was that I got to say thank you to my birth mother for my life. I also found out that Linda didn't live her life alone, which had been one of my fears growing up. She had gotten married and had three beautiful daughters. Even (not officially) "adopting in" a fourth. But when I began hearing about the not so good stuff it eventually became too much, and I shut down.

My intentions were good, and I know I did the best I could with what I had in that moment, but I was not equipped to handle the overwhelming emotions at that time. There was deep sadness, confusion, vicarious pain all topped off with the extreme guilt for wanting to know this part of my story. It was because of these emotional difficulties that I pushed myself away, and as she opened up, I shut down and hurt the person I had spent a great portion of my life wanting to thank.

By the time I was ready again, Linda's phone number had been disconnected, the address I had for her was no longer valid, and I couldn't find her. I had also moved and changed numbers, so she had no way of getting in touch with me. I carried a lot of guilt for many years about this, but I have found a way to forgive myself for this also.

Well, thank G-d for Facebook! In 2007, I was finally able to track Linda down again. Let's just say I was overjoyed to find her, and thankfully this was reciprocated. After about a year of communicating with her and my biological sisters, and positive that I was now 100 percent ready mentally, I booked a trip to meet everyone.

Have you ever had that 'aha' moment when everything just makes sense? That moment when suddenly you understand something, even if you don't really know why? That about summed it up! It was like all of a sudden understanding a language that I never spoke. During this trip there were many tears and many hugs—it was pre-COVID after all! There was also much learning and sharing. It was at this time that I was ready to hear Linda's story, and she was still willing to share it with me.

Linda had come from an extremely abusive background. She was the oldest of four children, two brothers and a sister. Her father was Metis and her mother Mennonite. At the hands of their father, Linda, her siblings, and mother all suffered unfathomable abuse—mental abuse, physical abuse, verbal abuse and sexual abuse. It is all recorded in a ground-breaking documentary that came out in 1987, called "To A Safer Place."

In fact, there is even a reference in it to the deformed baby who died—ME. I am not sure if the nurses told my biological mother that I was deformed under the blanket I was swaddled in, or if it was something she imagined, but given the fact that until a year ago she thought I was the result of one of those horrible rapes by her father, I am not surprised it is how she experienced it.

The circumstances around my conception were not the best. There is absolutely no question. At the time, Linda was seventeen, single and already had one child in foster care (does the word care here not seem ironic?). But what made someone else think it was their right to take her children from her? Although young, she did everything she could to take care of her son all on her own, even making the painful decision to put him into temporary care to make sure he would be provided for while she took care of the two of us. When she gave birth to me and wasn't even given a choice to be my mother and she was told I was going to die, the system took advantage of her. Burning questions fill my head—What kind of leadership allows this to happen? What kind of government allows this to happen? What kind of country allows this to happen?

I was blessed with a wonderful adoptive family, and parents who love me and still want, with all their heart, to give me everything I could ever want. I have two brothers that I have loved and tormented over the years, and who loved and tormented me right back. We always lived in a beautiful home, had plenty to eat and new clothes to wear. Education was important, and so were aspirations. Perhaps some people may be surprised at just how wrong I still feel this is given my semi-charmed kind of life, but how could I not feel this way?

I also need to take a moment here to make it abundantly clear that my parents had no idea that I was put into the adoption system illegally. They adopted me through the Jewish Child and Family Service, and they had no reason to question anything. As far as they were concerned, this was a standard adoption.

Yes, I absolutely do believe there were some strong psychological effects I suffered through because of all of this. Not feeling like you fit in, always searching, having abandonment issues, experiencing feelings of worthlessness—all these psychological effects took a toll on me. I felt intense loneliness, because I didn't feel that I could share what I was feeling with my adoptive parents. It wasn't because I couldn't talk to them, but it was because I didn't want to disappoint them or have them think my need to understand was an indication of a lack of love for them—that was the worst.

Here's the thing though… I have learned that stuffing things down doesn't work either. What you stuff down will not remain stuffed; it will eventually come out in different ways. Mine came out throughout my adolescence in the form of rebellion. For me, I was just trying to make sense of life and all the emotions that were swirling around inside. So many things were happening within because I was also trying my damnedest to fit in to a life that didn't really make sense to me. Though this is nothing compared to what Linda had to deal with, regardless, I have learned that it is okay to acknowledge your own pain, even when you think someone else's is worse. You can't move that pain or heal from it without acknowledging it and feeling it first.

I am in awe of Linda, my biological mother. She went from being abused by her father in the worst ways possible and being abused by a system and government yet carries the most amazing love and faith in her heart. We have all heard about intergenerational trauma, and I can tell you it is very real. The effects of losing her son carried forward and impacted my sisters' lives too. But I don't feel that's my story to tell.

Over the years, we had all been looking for that last missing piece, like a missing piece to a puzzle—where was our brother, my birth mother's son? I know it weighed heavily on Linda's heart. In fact, it weighed heavily on all of us. For the longest time, I felt responsible for my brother being taken away. I do know it is possible that it could have happened anyway, or that perhaps something else would have been the reason for him to be put into temporary care, but it wasn't, and silly or not, that was how I felt.

I don't think there was a time when one of us was not looking for our brother. It was during the summer of 2019 that I caught a break in the search for him. One of the people I had been following as a "potential brother" showed up in a picture on a Google search, with someone I knew. This was key for two reasons. Number one, I was able to find out this person's approximate age, which matched the age I knew our brother to be. Number two, I could now name drop. We knew someone in common, which I hoped would add a level of security when I reached out.

It was in August 2019, I sent David my first message. I had flagged his LinkedIn profile for some time but didn't really think I had reason to send a message. It was through this mutual person I had in common with David I got the courage to send a message introducing myself. I then asked two questions—was the birthdate I knew to be my brother's the same as his? and was he adopted? I had gone over so many different scenarios of what his response may be, but not once did I anticipate that he would never have been told that he was adopted. That was a whole other level of cannonballing someone's life that I had not given thought to.

I had not told Linda or my sisters that I suspected I found him yet, and this ended up being one of the hardest secrets I have ever had to keep, but for a short time, it was a secret that needed to be kept. Initially, David told me that he almost deleted that first message, and it was his wife who convinced him to look into it. In not knowing he was adopted, he had spoken with a lawyer who originally told him not to answer my message—this must be an elaborate phishing scam—but after being told my name, changed his opinion.

As it happened, I had been this lawyer's camp counsellor when he was at Winnipeg Beach Day Camp when I was sixteen. He was also friends with one of my other brothers (their sons are even friends). Knowing who I was, the lawyer knew I wouldn't have made this up. This was all David needed to agree to look into this. We both submitted our names to verify through the Adoption Registry that we were indeed biological brother and sister, and the rest is history.

I believe it was late September, early October of that same year (2019), when I could finally share the news with Linda and my sisters. Although I made it very clear to them that it was through all of our efforts we had found him, I'll let you in on a little secret—I am happy it was me. I was finally able to give Linda something that expressed the gratitude I felt for the gift of my life. I still don't know how she carried me for nine months, while thinking I was a result of a rape by her father.

I do not want my story to be looked at as a sad one, I do not believe any of us would want that. What I do want is for this to be a story of multi-generational resilience, strength and love. I also want it to be used to give voice and encourage others to share their stories.

Growing up in the Jewish community, I spent much time learning about the Holocaust. I have had the privilege of reading and hearing firsthand stories by many SURVIVORS that show how feelings of shame and victimization can morph into feelings of strength and survival, through the sharing of these stories. I believe the two worlds I have each one foot in could learn much from each other. As stories are shared, weights are lifted, feelings of guilt and shame released, finally allowing healing to begin. Through sharing our stories, we also give strength and encouragement to others to also come forward and begin their healing journeys. There is strength in numbers, and solace in sharing.

I have healed much over the past fourteen years. Some before finding David, and some after. Since finding him, I have also seen healing in Linda and my sisters. We all still have more to do on our individual healing journeys, but our circle is complete. Did David feel the things I felt growing up in a family that wasn't his biologically? How has this all affected him? Well, that's a story for him to tell, and he does in the next chapter. I do, however, suppose there is much truth to the saying, "Life takes you unexpected places but love always brings you home."

Blessings.

THE
"REC·ON·CIL·I·A·TION" OF DAVY

BY DAVID MORTIMER

It was 5:44 PM on August 28, 2019 when I received a LinkedIn message from a woman introducing herself as Lisa. It was an unusual message to say the least. One unlike the typical LinkedIn connection requests that invite you to build your professional network or try to sell you a new product or service. This message was very personal. It posed several innocent questions. The type that can shake you to your core and have you questioning everything you ever thought to be the truth.

Today, there is one constant in my life that remains true. I was born August 15, 1967 at the St. Boniface Hospital in Winnipeg. There is nothing remarkable knowing the day in which one is born. We take such personal information like our name, our heritage, our family, our history for granted and accept it all as our truth.

But what if these are not the truth and everything you ever believed about your childhood, family, culture, and heritage were shrouded by years of lies? What if… you are not the person you always believed you were? This has been my reality since receiving this LinkedIn message and what it had uncovered almost went undetected if it wasn't for a fifty-year search by a mother and family determined to find their truth.

Let me start from the beginning…

My family and I moved to Victoria in the late 1960s, roughly two years after I was born. While I do not have many memories of the five years we lived in B.C., I do recall the feeling of being trapped whenever engulfed by the thick fog rolling in from the shoreline and the surge of exhilaration when I had climbed a large cherry tree for the first time at a house we had just moved into as a family.

I was the youngest of three children and the only boy. My oldest sister was nine years my senior, my middle sister five years. My parents immigrated from Scotland with my oldest sister in tow. We had no extended family in Canada and I never knew much about the family we left behind in Scotland. It was a topic rarely discussed and to this day, I never met an aunt, uncle or cousin. I don't even know how many I had.

I did meet my maternal grandmother once when I was about fifteen. She made the trip to attend my middle sister's wedding—a wedding my father and oldest sister refused to attend. Such dysfunction was not unusual for my family. Truth is, we seemed to only know how to exist within the boundaries of silence, retribution, secrecy, and a twisted belief in loyalty one could only understand by living in a home that was cut off from friends and extended family.

A strong feeling I had growing up was that of being on the outside looking in at my life and never truly fitting within my family. A feeling that was hard to pin down, yet only grew in prominence as the years passed.

This was not difficult to conceive. My father was a forbidding man. He grew up in the Scottish military and was a boxer with an unset broken nose, missing teeth and tattoos that declared such things as *"Death before Dishonour."* He rarely spoke to me, but he always seemed to take delight tormenting me in front of my mother with some form of physical, emotional, or physiological test of being a man.

By the time I was fourteen, my father could barely acknowledge my existence. He refrained from looking or speaking directly to me. He simply communicated through my mother advising what "her son" should be doing to meet his expectations. Other times, without notice, communication came in the form of swift and highly unpredictable physical outbursts—only to return to the sound of silence, never to be spoken of.

I never knew the age of my parents. From a best guess, my mother was likely five years older than my father and would have been close to forty when I was born. She had a caring nature and a quick wit. However, she was also exceptionally secretive and rarely expressed her emotions. The years of isolation from her family, combined with the chronic strife and dysfunction took its toll on her, as she suffered with debilitating depression later in life.

I do recall a time when our relationship was close. However, this slowly eroded, as I could never truly compete with the closeness she had with my oldest sister. In fact, this was the one and only thing my parents ever had in common. Neither my middle sister nor I developed the same bond our parents had forged with our oldest sister. As a result, we developed a close relationship, despite being two very different people. She was sensitive, caring and compassionate, I was not. When we were young, she would often try to deflect my father's anger away from me, only to receive the blunt end of a verbal tirade for her attempted intervention. She too had endured her own trauma and despite leaving home when she was eighteen, she continued to hang on to the hope our family would one day reconcile, which only resulted in many more years of dysfunction and disappointment for her.

Life only got harder when my father lost his job in the late 1970s. Our family was struggling financially, and we moved once again, this time to Winnipeg's North End—a tough, inner-city neighbourhood. We lived in an old 1930s two-story home a block and a half off Main Street. I was now entering my fourth school in six years and had fallen far behind other kids my age. I was just starting to make some headway at school, finally understanding why I could hardly read. I was what they called "dyslexic." My father simply declared it as retardation.

I was now back to another school, another Special Needs Class and another round of reading *The Adventures of Dick and Jane*. Inevitably we spent more time playing floor hockey, as the class would degenerate into frenzied taunting and in-class scrimmages. School never got any easier despite my being pushed through the system into high school. Life in a large inner-city school with over 1,000 students offers an easy place to retreat to its shadowy corners. By grade eleven, I was hardly attending school and left without graduating—at least not this time around!

By the time I was seventeen, life at home was growing intolerable. My mother was breaking down under the strain of constant dysfunction. She was deeply depressed, isolated and stuck in a very unhappy marriage. This was not the first time she was struggling. She was hospitalized once before for her depression and had returned to Scotland with my oldest sister for several months when reaching another breaking-point when I was fourteen—I thought she may never return home. Truth is, I wish she had stayed in Scotland; she would have been far happier living out the remaining years of her life!

This time was different though. My mother seemed defeated and declared I was the most defiant, stubborn person she had ever known and wanted to know why I would not just accept my father? I was stunned by the question. Could she be right, was I the one that rejected him? Surely, if anyone knew the rejection I had endured, it would be her. It was clear, the tide had now turned, and it was time for me to figure out how I was going to leave!

A strong belief I had growing up was this notion I would not live a long life. I had this feeling as long as I can remember. It never presented as fear, in fact, now looking back, it seemed to create an independence and drive I used to plow through perceived barriers. As I grew older, I always felt I needed to do more than others and to do so with greater urgency. In some ways, this belief helped me overcome obstacles and let go of resentment, but it also came at a price of never allowing myself to be fully content, happy and satisfied.

The major turning point in my life came in the form of a pretty blonde girl (now my wife) and her family. We met and started dating several months before my eighteenth birthday in 1985. At the time, she was convinced I was part Native (aka Indigenous). A common belief by many at that time given the neighbourhood I came from.

The fact is I had many friends we now call Indigenous. In those days it was "Indians and Half-Breeds," and I was often thought of as the latter. This was something I never questioned or really cared about. Why would I? My parents immigrated to Canada, they both had thick Scottish accents and I was of the first generation to be born here in Canada.

After several months of dating, no steady employment and living on my own, I began working for my girlfriend's father. He owned a construction company, where I worked for a number of years; starting as a labourer, working my way to carpenter's apprentice and then project estimator. Over a period of time, he accepted me as a son, taught me a work ethic and encouraged me to return to school in the evenings and weekends, where I eventually completed my high school credits and later graduated from college and university.

By my early twenties, I was married and had switched my career to Financial Services. I had a son before turning thirty. My life was now worlds apart from where I had come. I was now with a family that accepted me, and my career was quickly advancing.

By this point, I rarely looked back at my childhood—the fact is, I buried most of it in the deepest recesses of my mind. However, I carried the heavy weight of shame for being rejected and not understanding the reason why. These feeling lurked below the surface, as there would always be constant reminders of this failure whenever I asked about my family or childhood.

The relationship with my parents and sisters all came to their own demise. We were deeply divided and fully estranged by the late 1990s. My son never met my father, nor my oldest sister who I have not spoken to since 1988. The relationship with my mother had unravelled after several attempts to salvage. She eventually became ill and died in 2007. We did not speak for almost ten years prior to her passing. She never did tell me about her illness, nor was I told when she died. My father-in-law simply phoned me with the news after reading her obituary in the paper. There was no funeral, no closure…just grief.

In some ways, my mother's passing proved to be the ultimate rejection, the ultimate failure of a son. This was something that stuck with me for many years as I tried to close that chapter of my life once and for all.

It was roughly twelve years after her passing when the August 28th message arrived. It was the Wednesday before the Labour Day weekend when I received an alert through my LinkedIn account from a woman, I did not know…

"HI David, this is going to be completely random but two questions…

Were you born August 15, 1967, and

By chance, were you adopted?"

She introduced herself as Lisa, saying she was adopted and looking to find her older brother. I was entirely skeptical; however, we did know a few people in common and she offered information that was not widely known to many people.

After two days of contemplating whether to delete this message, I finally showed it to my wife on the Friday evening. Her immediate reaction: "You need to respond to this message; it will offer you some answers." Answers to what I asked. "Maybe you are adopted David!"

Over that weekend, I learned a great deal from Lisa. She was adopted to a family I knew of by name in Winnipeg. She had a biological brother that was eighteen months older than her and if she was right about who I was, our birth mother, aunt and four sisters had been searching for me for many years.

The story was unbelievable! It read like fiction. I was taken from our mother shortly after she had given birth to Lisa, who was proclaimed deformed and not going to survive much longer. My mother was a fifteen-year-old girl when she got pregnant with "me" and was herself one of four siblings that were well known to the Children's Aid Society (CAS) of Winnipeg. They were a family in crisis and children of a Mennonite mother that was separated and seeking refuge from a very abusive French Canadian Metis father.

I did not sleep much that weekend; rather I traded numerous emails with Lisa, while at the same time searching the application process to the Manitoba's Post Adoption Registry. I also contacted my family lawyer for advice, who promptly met me Tuesday after the long weekend.

From there, things moved very quickly. Despite my lawyer's original advice not to engage with Lisa, believing it to be an elaborate phishing scheme, his advice quickly changed once he learned of her identity—declaring that he knew her as well as her adoptive family.

It was with my signed Post Adoption Registration that I made my way down to the Government Office on Portage Avenue. There I sat application in hand, waiting to meet a representative that would assist me with the discovery process...*and ultimately change my life forever.*

Since September 2019 I have learned many life changing things...

Firstly, I learned I was born Davy Turcotte on August 15, 1967 at St. Boniface Hospital in Winnipeg. I was raised by a very young mother for the first year of my life, where she attempted to care for me with little support and there were repeated attempts by CAS to apprehend me for adoption.

I entered the foster care system in August 1968 after my mother become pregnant and could no longer care for the two of us on her own. It was intended as a temporary placement, where we had routine visitations together as I moved between several foster families.

Provincial records indicate I was made a "permanent ward" by the province of Manitoba shortly after the birth of my sister. Visitations with my mother were immediately cut off and I was promptly moved to Victoria, B.C. in August 1969—not so coincidently to live with the first foster care family that had cared for me while in Winnipeg.

I was officially adopted by this family in January 1971, declared legal by the Supreme Court of B.C. My name was officially changed—bringing with it the demise of Davy Turcotte at the ripe age of three and a half.

I also learned my story is unfortunately not all that uncommon. These were standard operating practices routinely deployed by CAS Winnipeg during those years. I am just one, as is my sister Lisa, of thousands of Canadian children taken in what is now referred to as the *Sixties Scoop*.

It was a time where little regard was given to young unwed mothers, especially those with any trace of Indigenous heritage. The prevailing government of the day believed it was entirely acceptable to extinguish the identities of these children and to strip them of their family and heritage—even for those old enough to feel the bond of their birth mother!

I have learned life is not always what it seems. We become the stories we tell ourselves, even if those stories are built on lies. However, I have also learned the intuition we carry deep within us, even from a very young age can be remarkably accurate and offer some needed resilience.

As with Lisa, I too have learned life can take us to unexpected places, but it is love that brings us home. Our birth mother endured and overcame unbelievable hardships, yet she remains exceptionally loving. Despite losing two children at the age of seventeen, she married and raised a family of three additional daughters, later bringing in a fourth.

They too did not have it easy. They each felt the weight of their mother trying to reconcile the trauma she faced earlier in her life and had to endure in the years of searching for a brother they only knew by name, and continued to live in their mother's shadow.

Despite all of this, these women have accepted me fully into their lives without hesitation. A place where I now find myself healing as I continue this road of reconciliation.

I am now relearning my life's story in my *fifties* and trying to find ways that reconcile how best to integrate and honour Davy back into my life.

I am also learning what it is to be a son again and how to open myself fully in the acceptance of a mother's unconditional love. A love that is beautiful, yet difficult to comprehend. I am learning what it is to be an older brother of five amazingly strong women I now call sisters.

This is important work that takes time to nurture and grow.

I am learning "truth and reconciliation," and "systemic racism" are far more personal to me than what I would have ever thought imaginable. I am also learning the art of forgiveness—not just for a system that failed a young mother and her son, nor a family that became consumed by harbouring horrible lies, but also that of self-forgiveness, which is necessary for the deep-reflection one takes on a journey such as this.

Finally, I am learning Gratitude, the type of Gratitude that is fifty years in the making!

AGAINST THE ODDS

BY VONDA J. KNIPFEL

I was born during a blizzard in the family home on White Bear First Nation Saskatchewan, Canada, December 26, 1969. Tragedy struck my family less than a year later when my mother was killed. My siblings were dispersed to residential school or adopted out.

I spent some time at Fort San for tuberculosis. Always wondering about the scars around my ankles, I found out years later that the younger children in the hospital were often tied to their beds.

I was adopted along with my younger brother in 1972. The beginnings with a new family. New mom and dad and three new older brothers. Just like that, we became "The Scooped."

We lived as a family, a dysfunctional one, for about a decade in Shell Lake Saskatchewan. Things were rough in those years. I battled depression at a very young age. I'm sure my brother did as well.

We moved briefly to Moose Jaw in 1980. I finished my grade five at William Greyson Elementary School, but in grade six we were in a new town and a new school. We moved to Rockglen, Saskatchewan. There was nothing good about this time. Nothing at all. Physical discipline became the norm. My brother's screams of pain and terror still haunt me.

School was not fun. My brother had fetal alcohol syndrome, so his learning capacity was limited. There were many nights of him crying over his homework and our parents would get so frustrated with him. I often helped him behind their backs to save him from being spanked or worse. I on the other hand had no problem with the educational part of school.

Fast forward a year and my brother is no longer at their home. He was at Dale's House in Regina. I was alone. My depression worsened. My lifetime struggle with an eating disorder began. I started to experience racism at school. The first time I was called a squaw by a peer shocked me. It broke me further. The tipping point came when my older adopted brother's friend sexually assaulted me. The incident was brushed off by everyone.

I swallowed a bottle of prescription medication and was hospitalized shortly after. Death I craved. I was unafraid of it.

A few visits to a shrink and a forced injection messed with my head. I questioned whether these memories were real? Did these things really happen to me? I never really shared the experience with my adopted parents. It was all so confusing. I doubted my sanity. I needed my brother. For the first time in our lives, we were separated. He was my best friend, my confidante, my reason for living. No one cared. Once again, we moved.

I started grade eight at the Prince Albert Collegiate Institute (PACI) in the fall of 1982. One evening, while taking the family dog for a walk in a nearby park I was approached by a middle-aged white guy in a blue tracksuit. I remember the colour and the yellow stripe that ran down the sides. He followed me and tried to pull me into some bushes from behind. I was able to scramble through the lower bushes and run. My parents didn't believe me.

I wondered why they weren't helping me. I was just a kid. Why was no one protecting me? I started to display behavioural issues, skipping school and not going home. I didn't care. By October my parents had had enough, and two social workers came to the house and took me away. I never lived with my adopted parents again.

I completed my grade nine via correspondence because I lived in tiny Missinipe, Saskatchewan with a foster family. They made moonshine and homemade wines. I began my journey with alcohol. In Grade ten I was in a new foster home in La Ronge Saskatchewan. Once again I was in a new foster home, new town, new school, and new troubles.

In 1986, at the age of sixteen, I ended up being sent to Regina to serve an open custody sentence at Dale's House. My time in Regina was short, only three months. Just enough time to meet an amazing teaching assistant. She changed the whole game on my outlook on life. Thanks K.L. One month before my seventeenth birthday, my social worker dropped me off at the YWCA in Prince Albert. I was alone in the city.

In June 1987, I was a few months away from the arrival of my daughter. I was still a ward of the government and now they could potentially take my baby from me. My social worker took me to Martha House in Regina. There were other girls who shared my condition. While there, I met a mother figure who guided and protected me and was my advocate. Thank you, Sister Margaret.

Six months later, I turned eighteen and was officially free. It was terrifying. I took every parenting class available. It was in one of these groups that I happened to meet my older biological sister. What are the odds!?

In 1992, I went back to school, and later graduated with my grade twelve basic education. It was around this time that I slowly began to meet more of my biological family. I promised my kids and myself not to fall into any gangs or live a drug lifestyle. My brother promised me the same.

Over the next ten years I was a stay-at-home mom living on government assistance. I wanted more. I had held jobs before but nothing permanent. I always ended up back where I started. I was discouraged but I knew I couldn't give up, and that I had to keep moving forward. I also realized that I couldn't let fear stop me, because my children were watching and learning, and I had to be strong for them.

On January 15, 2004, I started my first day working at The Salvation Army Waterston Centre. I was cooking at a men's shelter. My first real job and I knew I didn't want to mess this up. Fast forward seventeen years and I am older and wiser. My children are grown, and I am blessed with thirteen beautiful grandchildren. Life is how I made it. I am a survivor.

My brother passed in December of 2016. I also lost my older biological brother and a younger half-sister earlier that year. I was present for their passing, and it changed me. Grief comes in waves. I break down and cry and know that's okay. I am thankful for every day that I wake up. I am still working at the Sally's. I am in a healthy eleven-year relationship with another amazing Scoop survivor. Thanks J. You've taught me so much.

I'm ready for this next chapter of my life. I know that I will be okay. I have a voice now and I use it often.

HIRAETH

BY D.B. MCLEOD

Hiraeth, *to be homesick or longing for a place that you have never been or can never return to.*

I have a Welsh word tattooed on my body. From what little familial stories I have, I do not have any Welsh ancestry. However, this word means so much to me. The first time I had read the word *hiraeth*, I burst into tears. My body longs for a place that I do not know, I am homesick for a place I have never been.

I was apprehended by the Children's Aid Society when I was three or four. The dates and ages changed with each story that I was told by the people who adopted me. I have a fairly vivid memory of that day. I was at daycare, there were a couple of adults that I didn't think I knew. They told me I had to go with them. First, these strangers took me to buy a blonde Cabbage Patch doll and a pizza, and then I was dropped off at "my new parents" house to play with my younger sister who was apprehended the year before.

I remember being finished playing with my little sister, turning to these adults and saying "Ok, I wanna go home now, I wanna see my mama." The adults said, "this is your home and this woman is your mom now." I remember feeling sad. A lot of people think it's weird that I have such vivid memories of when I was so young, but I think it's the trauma that has imprinted these memories onto my brain. Sometimes I think it is a cruel joke, and this is a part of my daily thoughts.

The social worker who handled our case was named Sue something. She wrote my sister and I letters about our birth parents. My younger sister and I have different fathers. Sue wrote non-identifying information about my parents. I recall my adopted father telling me a story about how he read these letters to my sister and I. I was around six or seven years old. He told me with a little more laughter in his voice than he should have had, that I cried when I was told I was Native.

My adopted father told me that my birth father is an Indian, and that I am half. Somehow even as a small child I knew that this meant different, not good enough. Even now as I write this, I am looking at a picture of me in kindergarten, I have a pink dress and pink barrettes, but even with all that pink and frill, you can see the straight dark brown hair, almond shaped eyes and brown skin.

Now as an almost forty-year-old woman, I look at this child and cry. I just want to hold that beautiful little girl and tell her it's going to be okay. I want to say to her, "No, you are not ugly it's the colonizer's gaze that made you feel this way," and, "No Denise, you aren't stupid, its racism. One day you are going to grow up and become a professor, you are going to go to graduate school, and one day you will find many people who will finally tell you how brilliant you are and tell you this often."

I want to also say, "No Denise, you are not too hard to love, you will find the people who will love you and they will love you so hard your heart will feel like it will burst from love. Initially when people treat you the way you deserve, it won't feel right, but those kind words and that love will heal the hard bits and make them soft."

It was in 1988–89 that the adoption papers were officially signed. I remember I had to sign the papers too; it wasn't as if I had any choice in the matter. I remember wanting to run far away from these people who were now my "parents." In this new home there was no love. No affection, no hugs or kisses or parents saying that they loved you. I don't remember a lot about my birth mother, but I remember she was loving. I guess my adopted parents tried in their own ways to love us. But even as a small child it was very apparent how much these two hated each other.

My adopted mother came from a very working-class family from Orillia Ontario, and my adopted father was from a middle class, very WASPY family from Toronto. These two people had nothing in common but decided to be married for twenty years. There were a lot of fights in our home. I remember that they would often get physically violent towards each other. While my adopted father was never physically violent with us, I also do not remember him showing us affection or love. My adopted mother, on the other hand, often abused us physically.

I have many memories of my adopted mother losing her patience with us and lashing out. Once while she was bathing me, I did something that she didn't like, and she shoved my head under the bath water and held it there for what seemed like an eternity. I often wonder if this abuse was the reason I was a shy kid who didn't talk much and latched on to any adult who showed me any sort of attention. My adopted parents had one last huge fight that lasted a few days, and it was very violent with both of them attacking each other. My adopted mother left the house, and my adopted father was left to fend for the three of us. I remember overhearing a phone call of my adopted father begging my adopted mother to come and get us. She did come and pick us up one summer day, and I didn't see my adopted father for eight years after that.

I spent eight years being terrorized by a woman who didn't really want to have children or at least not the children she adopted. I remember often being told that Indians were bad, lazy and all the rest of the typical stereotypes. I used to wish that I looked like the pretty, blonde-haired, blue-eyed girls that all the boys wanted to play with. I was eventually able to leave my adopted mother's house and move in with my adopted father and his new wife, my stepmother, who weirdly enough was also adopted. My stepmother tried to show love but because of her own trauma she was often mean. I spent my teenage years living on Sentinel Road in Toronto Community Housing, and spending hours in my room listening to the radio and dancing, dreaming of a life far away from my lived reality.

While Toronto gave me the ability to be ambiguous about my heritage, I longed to be a part of something. I would often go to the Native Canadian Centre for the Thursday Socials but wouldn't ever tell my parents where I was going. If they knew I would be ridiculed about being "Indian." My adopted father would tell "jokes" about all the worst stereotypes of Indigenous peoples. When I turned thirteen, my adopted father gave me the letter that the social worker Sue had written for me.

It turned out that *both* of my parents were Indigenous and not just my father. My world was rocked! My mother is of mixed Indigenous and Settler heritage. My father is from a reserve called Sagamok Anishnawbek First Nation, and both of my parents were involved in "care" as well. My father was placed in care on his reserve when he was three because both of his parents died. I would later find out when I met my birth mother that she was scooped from the hospital as a newborn.

I grew up in the 90s in Toronto, and the thing to do was to go "downtown." I would go to Queen Street West with my friends. We were always on the hunt for second-hand clothes, to prove how alternative we were. We would run through Kensington Market, a pack of wild teenagers. When we would walk by street-involved Indigenous folks, I could feel my body going numb as soon as we reached the Queen and Bathurst intersection. I would wonder, "Who would say what to me? Would the high cheek bones, brown, almond shaped eyes and long brown hair give me away to the folks sitting on that corner?"

Would they call out, "Hey sister, come here," or would it be my friends making some "joke" about drunken Indians, *not* seeing my long brown hair, high cheekbones, and brown, almond shaped eyes? It would take me *years* of unlearning and healing from all that internalized racism.

Almost a month after I turned eighteen, I put my name on the adoption registry to see if I could find a birth parent. Also, as my first act of freedom I got a tattoo and I moved out of my adopted father's and stepmother's house and in with my very first boyfriend, who I thought I would love forever. This shockingly turned out to not be true, and for that I will always be thankful.

When I put my name on the adoption registry, I was warned that it could take years to be matched with family. This was not true for me; I was matched with my mother within six months of putting my name on the list. At nineteen, I got pregnant with my first daughter, I had always wanted to be a mom and I was so excited. On my twentieth birthday I met my birth mother and was six months pregnant.

Looking back, I was not ready to meet her, I was not ready for a relationship with my birth mother. I was a kid who was getting ready to be a mother and had zero support from anyone around me. At the end of 2001, my first child was born, and she came out looking exactly like me. I was so shocked because I didn't think that anyone could look like me. I thought she was the most beautiful person in the whole world. I mean she is, but I am biased. I took my first-born to see my adopted mother a few times. She was excited to hold my daughter. When I was twenty-two (the same age my mother was when she gave birth to me) I gave birth to my second daughter and started my journey in post-secondary studies. It was around then when I lost contact with my birth mother. As I write this, I am toying with the idea of trying to find her again.

It took many years to find the strength to even think about looking for my birth father. I was twenty-eight. I was working in an Indigenous organization in Toronto's Regent Park neighbourhood. I had walked into my boss's office to talk about something but found myself getting up the nerve to ask how I could start looking for my father. She asked his name and where he was from; I gave her all the information I had. She sat quietly for a moment and then said, "I am going to call my friend who is from your reserve."

She called her friend and engaged in small talk for a few moments and then she said, "I have a young woman that works at my organization, she is an adoptee, and her father is from Sagamok." She gave my father's name, said, Ok here is her number. Ended the conversation with some well wishes and goodbyes. It was after she put the phone down that she then looked at me and said, "My friend says that he knew your father and that they both grew up in the same foster home and that your father was a very sweet and kind boy." She ended the conversation with, "My friend is giving your number to your father's siblings. Just wait, someone will call you."

I waited, for about four months. On February 19th, 2010, the kids and I were getting ready to go to a Valentine's day dance at the Native Canadian Centre, when I got a phone call from a random 705 number. I answered the phone and the whole world fell away. It was the call I was waiting for. I recall the conversation as though it happened just the other day. My cousin spoke first: "Hey can I speak to Denise please?" and I answered him with

"This is she." (I was raised by white people. I have weirdly polite phone etiquette)

Cousin: So, hey, this is Mathew, Angus is my uncle.

Me: Oh hey! That means we are cousins! Thanks so much for calling! I was looking for my father, can you give him my number?

Cousin: So, um, well I cannot do that.

Me: Oh, he doesn't want to talk to me? Okay thanks for letting me know.

Cousin: No it's not that, um, well he died.

Me: Oh.

Cousin: Um, yeah he died on February 12th, last week. Tomorrow is the funeral. You are welcome to join.

Holding back tears, I said, "Oh, um, thanks for letting me know, I won't be able to make that." My cousin gave me my auntie's number and told me I could call her. Fighting back more tears I told my cousin, "Thank you so much, take care and thanks for calling." My cousin and I said goodbye and the phone call ended.

I got off the phone and crumpled to the floor, wailing. My daughters ran up to me while I was sitting on the floor distraught and asked, "Momma what's happening?" I replied between sobs, "My father passed away last week." My daughters sat with me on the floor hugging me and telling me, "It's going to be Ok."

After a few minutes, I told them we were going to the Native Centre. The rest of that night is a blur because I don't recall what happened. A few days later I braided my hair and cut it off, saving the braid in my sock drawer. I did not take time off of work to mourn, I did not even really address it. I didn't think it was appropriate that I mourn a stranger.

This culminates in me, a month later, getting *very* drunk and throwing up on my favourite boots outside of a convenience store at Dundas and Dufferin. I cried in my friend's lap and asked over and over, "Why didn't he love me?." I called in sick to work the next day and my boss spoke to my friend about what is going on with me. My boss then kindly but assertively got me into counselling.

Maybe a month after my father's death, I called my auntie. She is very sweet, and we talked a little. She told me about our clan, our family, and the reserve. She asked me to come up, but I didn't feel ready. We talked for about a year and then in 2011, for a work trip I was on Manitoulin Island.

A co-worker told me on a Sunday morning, "Denise, it's time to go home" and then started the drive to Sagamok. I called my auntie, "Hey, I am going to be dropped off in Sagamok in one hour, will you be home?" She excitedly said, "Yes I will be home, I will see you soon."

I sat in the back of the van as my co-worker and I quietly drove to Sagamok. I was unsure what to expect and I was nervous. As we drove up to the Sagamok sign, I got out and took pictures in front of it like a tourist. I now cringe at this action. We drove all the way up to the top of the hill to my auntie's place at the Elders lodge. We pulled up and I got out of the van. My co-worker yelled, "I will see you in four hours," and drove away. I was terrified.

What is this little urban Nish woman doing on the Rez? My auntie came out of the building and hugged me. With this hug I felt full, like the empty part of my body filled with love. I looked at her. She looks like me or rather I look like her. I look like people! I am not this oddity that looks like no one, as if born from an egg.

For the next four hours, my auntie took me around the community and introduced me to family. There was a lot of Anishinaabemowin spoken around me, none of which I know. I realized these strangers were connected to me, and that we shared the same DNA. They also stared at me, and asked me the same series of questions, in Anishinaabemowin and then in English, when I stared at them blankly.

"Did Angus know about you?"; "Where do you live?"; "How did you find your dad?"; "Where is your mother from?" Questions I answered repeatedly.

Finally, my auntie took me to a little house, and while we were walking into the kitchen, I noticed that there was a beautiful Indigenous woman who was melting down Crisco to make fry bread. My auntie and this beautiful woman had a conversation in Anishinaabemowin, and during the whole time this beautiful woman was staring at me.

When this mysterious woman finally acknowledged me, she also asked me a lot of questions. "So did your dad know about you?" I replied, "Yes, but it was the early 80s and he couldn't be a dad."

"So you live in Toronto, what do you do?" I told her about my work and what I did in the city. I then remembered to show people pictures of my daughters. I took out my phone and said, "These are my daughters."

This woman took my phone and stared at the pictures for a while and then said, "I grew up with your dad, he was a very kind boy. I hope you know that he would be so proud to have such a beautiful daughter and granddaughters."

I was taken aback by these statements and tried not to cry in this woman's kitchen. I whispered my thanks and rushed out of the house. I cried as the sun beamed down on me. I was finally on my ancestral homelands.

I visited my father's grave and talked to him. I put a stone on his headstone the way I was taught by my stepmother. I said goodbye to my auntie and newfound family and my co-worker came and picked me up. Driving back to Manitoulin Island, my body felt a newfound fullness and lightness that I had never experienced. As I fell asleep that night, it was the happiest I had been in years.

That May weekend was ten years ago. It was the beginning of my healing journey and the beginning of my learning journey. Finding home was a needed step in the process of finding my voice, being comfortable in my skin and unlearning all those years of hurt inflicted on me by the people who adopted me.

I have chosen to not have a relationship with the people who adopted me because I don't want my children to grow up with feelings of shame about who they are. I have been able and privileged to teach my daughters about who we are as Anishinaabe people. I have cultivated a beautiful chosen family in Toronto, and my daughters have so many aunties that they are learning from. I am happy that they have such amazing role models.

I have been able to learn about Indigenous Birth Work and sing to the babies when they arrive from the spirit world. I have learned how to sew moss bags and bonnets, ribbon skirts and shirts. All of this has been so healing not only for me, but I believe that I am also healing the generations of ancestors that have also been displaced or weren't able to receive or share these ways of knowing and being.

I now have become an auntie for my community. This honour is one I do not take lightly. I have learned how to make "the best bannock and scone" and cook traditional foods. I try to walk and do things in a good way and take directions from my own aunties, both blood and the ones who have adopted me into their families.

While this journey of reclamation was long and painful, I often remind myself that where I am right here and right now is the best place to be.

THE MATHEMATICS
OF MY LIFE

BY SHAUN LADUE

When I look back over my life, I have come to realize that my biological family has endured the "perfect storm." My parents attended the Lower Post Residential School in the 1950s. Three of my biological siblings also attended the same residential school.

In 1967 when I was born there was a change in the assimilation process by the government—one of my brothers and I became part of the thousands of children who were taken away from parents to be raised by white Canadians. In early January 1970 my mom became one of the thousands of Murdered and Missing Indigenous Women and Girls.

Being a residential school survivor, and watching her family being broken up due to Governmental interference had led my mother to drink and not trust herself and ending up with a man who didn't value her.

Residential School [2]
+ MMIWG
+ Sixties Scoop
_____

= A messed-up childhood, adolescence and an interesting adulthood [2]

I knew very young that I was adopted—my adoptive parents had blue eyes and pale skin, whereas I was dark—dark hair, dark eyes, and dark skin. I remember when I would come home from school excited to have made a new friend. Once I told my mom who my new friend was, she would get very angry and tell me to never play with that child again. I didn't know at the time, but many of these so-called unsuitable friends were actually my cousins and relatives. I didn't know I was being raised in the town with my biological relatives. I didn't know that three of my siblings were attending Lower Post Residential School just twenty-three kilometres south of where I was being raised.

My only connection to my biological family was my brother Terry, the second youngest. He continued to live in the foster home where I had been for the first three years of my life. We had a tight bond that the adults in our lives tried to downplay or break. My adoptive mother didn't like him, and she had fears that he would come and take me away one day.

The Sixties Scoop mandate was to give Indigenous children to white Christian families so the children would grow up with a work ethic, with religion and to be colourful white folks. Instead, many of us grew up very confused, angry at those who raised us and angry at ourselves for being born Native. I also had a small complication; I knew very young that I was queer. At the time I didn't know the exact word. It wasn't until I was in my forties that I began to live my life as authentically as I could.

Before I could begin to truly enjoy life at the age of forty-five, I had to go through many years of intensive therapy to basically undo all the cruel messages given to me during my childhood. The biggest and most hurtful message was that I didn't deserve love. That message came not only from the adoptive parents, but from other family members and other community members. To this day, I cannot comprehend what a person is thinking when they tell a small child they don't deserve love.

I had to break down every message I had received, toss out the hurtful negative bits and begin loving myself and then I had to parent myself. It was a lot of hard work. Fortunately, I had some great people in my life who were patient and continued to shower me with unconditional love when I faltered.

Is this what the government intended? To have a generation of broken adults who felt they neither fit in with their biological families or their adoptive families' cultures? And for those who found success in bridging between their two families and cultures—congratulations, I am truly happy for you. For those of us who haven't, what do we have? Broken connections, a huge sense of dislocation and a huge sense of loss.

I found that developing a family of the heart has been the most healing. These are others, regardless of race, age, ethnicity who are very important to me—they take on roles of aunties, grammas, uncles, sisters, and brothers. They don't judge me because of the colour of my skin, or the fact that I am queer. They care about how I feel, about what kind of day I am having, or what is making me laugh today. They check in to make sure I remember I am loved , that I am important and that I am a valued member of their family.

I found that because I am Indian, Native, Indigenous, Aboriginal, First Nations—whatever term society tosses our way—they try to get each of us to squeeze into a tiny box of conforming, so we make society comfortable. As I healed from the years of abuse, neglect, and racism, I tossed that little box of what society thought a good Native person should be into the fire. I am here to live my life as I see fit. If I don't hurt others, as long as I respect others, I can live as I like.

As a young person just leaving foster care, I relied on an adult I trusted as to what my adult life should look like. She painted a picture of: get an education, get married, have kids, buy a house.

Education
+ Marriage
+ kids
+ a home
_____
≠ HAPPINESS

I started down that path; after five years, I wasn't happy. Nothing she pointed to made me truly happy. I had the education (a Bachelor's degree in education), but I left my spouse, didn't have any kids and didn't buy a house. I roamed for a few years. I taught overseas in South Korea, and when I returned to Canada I taught at an alternative high school for Indigenous students.

This was when I started to struggle with memories. Things that had happened to me as a kid were flooding back and, in the beginning, I was desperate to hide from them and to get them to go away. But these memories kept coming. I had to leave my position as a teacher and seek help. It took some time to find someone who would work with me, as many of the counsellors I went to see couldn't get over the fact that I was educated, that I didn't have any addiction issues or criminal issues. It hurt that they had a limited view of who First Nations people were. Yes, there are a lot of First Nations people who deal with addictions issues and other social issues, but it's not true of all First Nations people.

I have been fortunate not to have developed a taste for mind-altering drugs. The therapist I found was a doctor who was originally from South Africa and it seemed like she didn't have the same racist conditioning I had experienced from other therapists. We worked intensely for three years, and when I was done, I had my life back. The memories and messages of my childhood were disarmed and no longer scared me.

Flooding Memories
– Coping Skills
+ Highly Skilled Therapist
───────────────────────────
= Healing, becoming Healthy and Strong

As I found my strength to live, I discovered that the queerness that was hidden under all my pain and anguish erupted in all its rainbow glory. In the years between my young adulthood and my middle age the words to describe my queerness had caught up with my experience: transgender, pansexual, and polyamorous. Transgender is when a person's gender identity doesn't match their biological sex. Pansexual is a sexual attraction to another person's heart, mind and soul and their gender identity doesn't really matter. And Polyamorous is having sexual and romantic relationships with multiple people. It's more complicated than that, but those are the basic definitions. At the age of forty-five I began my transition and within a few years my physical body was more aligned with how I saw myself.

```
┌─────────────────────────────┐
│                             │
│  Transgender Yukoner        │
│  + Polyamorous              │
│  + Pansexual                │
│  ─────────────────          │
│  = Two Spirit Person        │
│                             │
└─────────────────────────────┘
```

I had been living in Vancouver and decided to return home to the Yukon to develop relationships with my biological family and to reconnect with other friends and family. I began to challenge myself by building an off-grid tiny house in my home community and learning more construction and carpentry skills. These three years were a lot of fun. Every morning I would wake and stare at the ceiling mesmerized that I was living in a house that I built. That alone was so empowering.

Unfortunately, things went a bit sideways when someone stole my dog. She was my family and my companion. That really hurt. There were other things that were happening, the social issues in my home community were overwhelming—the alcohol abuse, and the incoming drugs like crack, and seeing so many people struggling. I decided to move to my sister's family homestead in the Southern Lakes area. I also decided to become more nomadic. I loved travelling and it made sense to find a trailer and hit the road during the winter.

At the age of fifty-three, I feel like I am finally living my life in the best possible way. I have family, some are biological, some are fosters, some are people who have wormed their way into my heart, and I love them all dearly. I am now more or less nomadic. I spend my summers in the Yukon, and the rest of the year is spent travelling—I have driven across Canada and a lot of the United States and I am making more plans to get out and do more.

My regret? My only regret was that it took so long to heal from the abuse. I am glad I did it, but I look back over those fifteen years and miss what could have been. Would I do it again? Yup! I know myself thoroughly, and I know my strengths and how to use them to make every day a good day.

Knowing Myself
+ Family of the Heart
+ Goals and Dreams
+ Being Nomadic
———————————————
= The Best Version of Me

A LETTER TO MY SISTER

BY CHRISTINE MISKONOODINKWE SMITH

As a Sixties Scoop survivor, I often learned to misplace my anger, and would put it on people in situations that I could better control. I had no control over the actions of my adoptive parents, so I learned to put it on the next closest person to me. Nisaakihaa nimihsens (I love my sister).

There's an anger inside that I feel towards you. I have never really been able to put my finger on it. I think the answer is there, but it chooses to hide within my subconscious just waiting to rear its ugly head, especially I when I feel the littlest of slights from you.

This anger, though, is very real. It was there when we were children, and you got all the attention from our adoptive parents, and I was shoved aside and was threatened to keep silent. It was there, when the slightest of behavioural infractions was caught, and I took the brunt of the punishment, even though I hadn't done anything.

You were considered the angel and I was the devil incarnate. I remember in grade three, when out of the blue, I was yanked from our grade school, and made to go to another grade school ten mere minutes away from where we lived. I was told "it's for your own good," but was it really?

We both misbehaved according to their standards, but I was the one who silently took the punishment. Just like the flavour of the month—it meant a beating, staying home and being the dutiful daughter who cleaned the house from top to bottom and missing a hot dog day at school. Hot dog days at school happened to be one of my favourite days—I don't really know why, just the thought of them now make me feel sick. I remember our adoptive parents making me eat them for a month afterwards—all because I had told you I was upset for missing that day.

Hot dog days at school allowed me to experience the joy of having hotdogs and ketchup just like my classmates. It meant not having to stick to the goddamn awful diet of white bread with peanut butter and jelly, sliced into four little squares—sandwiches that were made to look like they were made so lovingly. I knew the anger behind the person who made them. The person who quite blatantly told me at the age of six, "You're a little bitch."

There's an anger inside that I feel towards you. I have felt this anger all my life but have kept it as hidden as much as I possibly can. People who don't know my truth and what lurks beneath its surface, tell me, "You're lucky to have a sister."

They don't understand my silence after those words are said, the tears that fall later after they leave, or the discombobulation I endure afterwards when I am home all alone, trying to make sense of why? Why do I feel such anger towards someone I should have feelings of love for? I wonder if that was our adoptive parents' intention, to drive a wedge between us—two sisters who understood each other and the pain we learned to endure at their hands.

No one really understands the anger or the hurt that hides beneath the surface—the anger I can't let go of because I always knew that you were the one who was always wanted, and I was quite blatantly told, "You were never wanted, you were just a part of the package deal."

There's an anger inside that I feel towards you. I don't know if I will ever be able to understand it, let alone have you understand it either. I'm a grown woman now, and I should feel differently, but it's the verbal and emotional scarring of knowing you were wanted, and I wasn't, that will subconsciously always stay with me.

GOOD GIRLS
DON'T DO THAT

BY KAREN ORSER

Upon seeing the opportunity to submit our stories, I knew I wanted to try.

At first, I judged myself as this narrative came out, because I'm middle aged and can reflect on things a lot differently now. Then I sat back and let my mind find the story of the Sixties Scoop survivor. Life has many layers, thank you for letting me share one of mine, nakummek, akaluk!

Before ever understanding much about the world, I was often paraded around to friends and relatives, and they would declare how exotic and beautiful I was to my grandparents. "What do you want to be when you grow up?" I would search my grammy's face and I would reply, "A ballerina," followed by their smiles and then they would declare me the cutest. My aunty would roll her eyes. But it was a lie; I really wanted to be a stewardess on an airplane because some of my earliest memories were of these smiling, beautifully dressed women giving me blankets and cookies. I could imagine being so smartly dressed donning a spiffy hat and silky scarf around my neck, flying all over the place and always having cookies for lunch. But good girls don't do that. My dad named me after the then famous Prima Ballerina; I should want to be like her.

My adopted sister (six years my senior and my biological aunt) joked with her friends that when I'd arrived for good at three years old, I was a handful for her mother. She assigned regular naps and all sorts of foreign foods to be eaten and I wouldn't have any of it at first. Aunty remembered me turning one day amid a lecture, pointing to my grammy and shouting, "You bitch!"

It was soon that I found myself eating beans, watching Sesame Street, and going to Sunday School in the community church to memorize things. And remembering if I tried that line again my grammy had a slipper waiting for me, "I wasted too many good spoons on your father's behind, I'll not waste any on you; good girls don't do that!"

I was given an anti-depressant to help me with my bedwetting and my inability to accept the answer that my mother was never coming back, no matter how many times I asked. I asked for many years, even if it angered them all. I finally gave up when I was nine and not because I had found peace. My parents did come to visit me, and it was explained to me that they'd been teenagers when I was born and foolishly thought getting married would help. I'd heard it all, how my mother was difficult, and my father lost his temper and beat her up and went to jail.

Alone, my mother couldn't cope. Her own mother was also caring for many adopted grandchildren and encouraged her to talk to my other grandparents. It was the Inuit way. The trouble was they left Frobisher Bay for the Halifax area and this meant making the trek to Nova Scotia to make this happen. Twice my mother changed her mind and would fly to get me. My grammy explained this was no good for me and if they took me again, there would be adoption papers and I would be staying. She did do the adoption papers and there were no more stewardesses for a very long time.

My parents were like movie stars to me, always in modern clothes and bearing a toy even if Grammy scolded them about spoiling me. There were fun trips and lots of hugs and I'd fool myself into thinking they had changed their minds, but then there were terrible trips to the airport when they left without me.

My dad brought pretty ladies with him, potential wives coming to meet me. I was their test. It was not overly common in the mid 70s to have a mixed-race child in Nova Scotia; it was a hard test. Eventually one did stick and I'm happy to say she accepted the proposal; I got to be the flower girl and even sewed my own special dress.

My mother took longer but she did indeed show up when I was nine with a tall handsome man she married, and they were enjoying their honeymoon. They'd stopped on their way to Newfoundland where my mom would meet her new in-laws. She told my grandma she wanted to buy me new school clothes and I was thrilled because my grandparents didn't believe in getting new clothes for a growing child. Being raised the eldest of their siblings on farms in the Depression, they thought that was much too frivolous, and they felt it would surely spoil me. This was a phrase that would become ingrained in me. It was regularly repeated, as I grew. I did end up getting the clothes and going to the beach, twice! It was afterwards that a darkness descended upon my world.

My mom asked Grammy if I too could go to Newfoundland with them to meet her new husband's parents. I had no idea where that was, but I heard the resounding *no!* and the heated argument between them that ensued. I hid, I cried hot tears wondering why, again, was it *not allowed*. My mom eventually came to me and stooped down to look me in my face, she had to go, and she would never be back, she couldn't stand that bitch anymore she muttered. They left and I didn't feel tears anymore; I was angry, and I wanted answers. I was tired of being shoved out the room because the adults were talking, and I needed to know why I wasn't allowed. I was a good girl! I hadn't been bad, I really wanted to go, and my mom's new husband was so nice! *Why*?! She just said she was never coming back!

My grammy had no slipper this time; she was crying too. If there was one thing she tried, it was to tell me of my situation with my parents—as she saw it anyways. My mom couldn't be trusted, and she felt she had plans to take me back to Frobisher Bay instead of back to Nova Scotia and that was illegal. She didn't believe my mom's promises and my mom let her know it was wrong, because my dad took me places and he wasn't mistrusted. She was reminded by my grandmother: He doesn't drink. There were many more details I didn't hear, the anger inside of me blocked it out.

What was the deal with the drinking? My grampy and his WWII friends did it all the time and he took me places. He often bought me ice cream while he went in the Legion for a while, and I had to wait in the car. I knew mom wouldn't steal me; she didn't want kids, but I knew my words were useless, good girls didn't talk back and I'd already pushed my luck. I'd been through this many times and no matter what I wanted, it wasn't allowed. I was theirs and they had the adoption papers, and that was the final answer. They would tell me, "Stop crying before I come over there and give you something to cry about." I didn't understand that they were already breaking the rules that the judge and social worker had given them. I wouldn't see these papers for a couple more decades.

Life moved on. I had school, after-school clubs and friends, but they were all reviewed and allowed or denied. Sunday School, check, choir okay. Karate and band were approved if my marks were good. Now there was an incentive to get me to study, I hated being in that house.

My grammy was always "sick" and had to lie down; she was going through the change of life, and it affected her health and her moods. I tiptoed around, followed orders and did favours in attempts to make her happy. But there was no one formula that ever worked, my grampy was just as much of a victim as me, my aunty and my uncle.

Grampy often allowed a confused me onto his lap. He was quiet, calm. It helped me. We spoke to each other with hand gestures because if Grammy heard us, there would be more yelling and accusations. So, sports, band practice and sleepovers with friends got me through many years. Her frequent naps were helpful; they brought peace and we could talk and move and laugh without paranoia.

My dad and stepmom continued their bi-yearly visits. I even spent the summer in Hay River with them. I was in heaven there, I had choices and no slipper! The airplane ride was icing on the cake. They would send me home and tell me again how they'd love to keep me but couldn't break my grandparents' hearts. I always wondered, What about my heart? After returning, things seemed worse because there was more arguing, and more drinking which would lead to more arguing. My grammy started taking more trips to see her friends and relatives in New Brunswick. Her parents were getting fragile and needed her help. I was terrified of them, because I was always lectured about how I had to act before we went there. Once I was dressed right, I would be reminded I'd probably have to attend the scary Pentecostal church on Sunday. Their house was always so clean, but it smelled dusty. I was given regular reminders about not speaking unless I was spoken to. But at the end of the day, my fear really came from my grammy, because she was terrified of them, and she wasn't scared of anyone else. So, I thought this had to be bad right? I learned that they disapproved of her marriage because she'd gotten, "in the family way" with my uncle. From my point of view, adults seemed complicated. I was relieved to leave and visit cousins instead.

When my aunty started dating, she got her own room after my uncle married and moved out. I wasn't interested in how her friends and her hid away giggling about kissing boys—yuck! One day, while snooping in my aunty's room, I found her Playgirl magazine. I'd never seen a naked man before and my curiosity overrode my fears of being caught. I was reading crazy stories when my grampy found me.

My face hot with shame, he laughed. I was frozen in total shock; I wasn't in trouble. He gently told me this was normal; that I would get older and want to do these things. He laid down beside me and wanted to see the pages. He was hugging me too close and smelled of booze, I froze right up, and wanted nothing to do with this book anymore.

He was talking to me, describing how women really liked it, how it felt good and tried to show me some stuff. I was humiliated beyond measure, and I began crying. The tears kept coming. He finally noticed and took his lips off my body parts and assured me I'd like it one day and I could come to him anytime.

My mind was reeling from what had just happened. The world stopped, and I knew I would never be the same. I had no one to tell because if I did say anything, my grammy would know I had read this sinful and forbidden book. My aunty would also find out that I had snooped in her private things. The friends I had barely accepted me, and if they found out I knew they would surely never invite me over again. This would simply be the straw that broke the camel's back. Good girls don't do that. But worse, my mentor, my only ally in this house had just become a total stranger to me and I would never trust him again.

But in those moments and the months and years that followed, I was in no position to buck the system. I was eleven years old when it happened and was not able to leave or fend for myself yet. I was trapped in my brain, scared in my home, and wondered, What I could do? I didn't know how to deal with what had happened, so I just coped the best I could.

I continued to focus on school because that was something I could control. Continuing to excel and receive honours allowed me the liberty and rewards to be free from the house and away from the people I suffered such a love/hate relationship with. But it all began to overflow like water out of a clogged toilet.

I suffered with anxiety, insomnia, and bulimia. I began reading more and talking less. School remained an escape, but my girlfriends wondered why I didn't crush on boys like they did. My summers at the little cottage by the beach were good with my grammy, because while she napped, I walked a lot on the beach, daydreaming and finding shells. Sometimes I walked far out to the Point, where the cove ended and the open sea began and looked far as I could see, and wondered what was out there? I would question whether I would I always live in this jail that I felt I was in.

As I entered my teens, along came more rules. My peers went to concerts, got perms and boyfriends. I admired my friends, but I felt nothing but ugly inside and didn't believe any compliments that came my way. I excelled at martial arts, band and even joined basketball. I soon learned that the other girls didn't want me there because they'd been working as a team already. But even though the coach could tell I worked hard at practice, and he warned me that I'd just warm the bench for games I didn't care. Basketball practice at school meant less time at that house. Until *he* retired.

My grampy, getting older and suffering health issues finally retired. He got bored and would drink more. The drinking would lead to more fights, but my grampy had learned the presents to buy to get my grammy to make things better. Then, practice was over, and the games began. The question of whose parents could help with driving became my undoing.

Grampy had nothing better to do and he was thrilled to volunteer to get out of the house. Next thing I knew, he was the new team hero, and the girls cooed over him, thinking that he was so cute! He had a dozen giggling teenage girls fawning over him; he suddenly had lots of gas money and treats for my friends. I suddenly hated basketball.

When my aunty finished nursing school, she came home and found work. She bossed her boyfriend into wedding plans. She had goals, she was moving out, she'd had enough, and I was so jealous. But her boyfriend had a change of plans because his girlfriend was expecting. My aunty's heart was broken.

My father and stepmom who were home for this event said, "Hey, come stay with us out west, forget about him." There are better jobs, and you can have a new start. I couldn't go, but *she* could. Leaving me alone here? With him? Dad apologized; he couldn't break his parents' heart. Same tired words to my old, tired heart. I was never getting married, I thought.

I began to worry less about being a good girl and was textbook lashing out. My marks dipped down, I began to sneak out to have drinks and smokes with friends. I stopped worrying about the friend approval list and found new friends at the nearby Reserve. It felt liberating to speak to kids that were brown like me, who were unheard by their parents who drank too much and made them wear second-hand clothes. I was home. But this was not met with any joy by my grandparents or neighbours. I heard things like Wagon Burner for the first time, girls I knew since kindergarten stopped inviting me to the sleepovers so much. I started getting grounded, and my grammy would lament and say, "After all we've done for you!"

So, I brought my marks up, lied about sleepovers, and ran off to the Reserve instead. I received lectures, my dad would be called and I would get grounded again. Grampy tried to assure me that I could confide in him, invited me to his bed for cuddles, and bought me tobacco. It made things worse and one day I just blurted out, "I want to live with my dad."

My grammy was in disbelief and tried to tell me that I didn't mean it, and if I did then I would have to tell Grampy myself. She didn't know he'd long ago broke our bond and figured if I could tell him to his face, I meant it. It wasn't easy for the reasons she'd imagined, I hated finding myself alone with him, but I did it. He just hung his head and told me it was Ok; he didn't blame me for being tired of hanging out with old people.

I finally felt free. I bided by all the steps I was asked to make this happen. I made the declaration in the early spring but had to finish school first before living with my dad could happen. My friends were saddened, but I wasn't, I forged ahead. My aunty and stepmother arrived for a visit and then we bussed it back to Edmonton, Alberta. We then drove seven more hours to Peace River country and at last I found my new home. My elation was short lived; my dad had become convinced that I was just spoiled by living with my grandparents and doubled down on rules. There was no band, no martial arts, and if I needed money, I had to get a job after school.

My dad had suffered after a surgery to remove a benign brain tumour. At first, I didn't understand how, but learned quickly about the brain damage that he incurred. He had seizures, a short temper and had difficulty finding work as a heavy-duty mechanic. He eventually settled on truck driving, but as these details unfolded, I became convinced my family was cursed.

I wondered, how could I see other teens living their lives, going on vacations, and scoring cute boyfriends, while I had a part time job to help support my family. I still burned with shame when a boy showed an interest in me?

My mother caught wind of these changes and wanted to see me again. Family friends agreed to give me a ride to Fort Smith where she was living. She had a surprise; a new husband and she'd finished college. Everything was good, until after supper when her husband rolled a joint and offered me some. I declined. Drinks came out, again I declined. This earned me a new nick name—Holy Roller.

After calling my dad, I left the next morning. He was disappointed but not surprised. I understood I needed to finish high school and get on with my own life, without this family.

Where did I go? What did I do? I fled to Edmonton for the summer, and I finished vocational training to work on an ambulance. I found part time jobs and made lots of bad choices. I hung out with bad guys and got abused. I was followed by other men wanting to buy sex.

I later understood how fortunate I was to not have disappeared or have been murdered. But I just didn't get how a smart lady could attract such losers? I worked hard, didn't drink, minded my manners, kept a clean house, and could even cook. I puzzled my family, and they would often sigh on the other end of the phone, and I would hear, "You made your bed, now lie in it."

Eventually, my mom and I reconnected. It was always a rollercoaster ride with this woman. She'd call and we would chat for an hour, and it would be awesome. Then she'd call at one in the morning, drunk and yelling, blaming me or my dad for her problems. But then one day I received a fateful phone call. Her mother was sick with cancer and was possibly going to die. If she bought me a ticket, would I go visit?

Now that was a total shocker; I had grandparents. Cousins? I'd never imagined this because of our abrupt cut in visits when I was nine. At first I was angry and refused and wondered why I should care about people who'd abandoned me. My mom, embarrassed, explained they couldn't speak English and couldn't have called or written because they were poor. Okay, I thought; my mind was blown with this new knowledge. I agreed and dates were set.

I learned I would travel to Iqaluit, and not Frobisher Bay. What a game changer. My cousins met me at the airport with smiles and talked a mile a minute as they loaded me into a taxi. My grandparents were waiting for me at their home and burst into Inuktitut. I totally didn't understand but their gestures were clear, they hadn't seen me since I was little. I met aunties and uncles and more cousins every day. If my older cousin wasn't about, I needed the three-year-old so I could convey any needs to my grandma. She was very sick, but the good news was, with treatments, she would recover. I left, feeling grown up finally at twenty-one years old. A new light within me grew because I saw how much I was missed, and how much I was loved just the way I was.

At twenty-two years old, I became pregnant, and the father wasn't there to help me out. My aunty wrote my grammy letters accusing me of being a drama queen, and always needing attention. She even wrote that I got myself pregnant on purpose so everyone would feel sorry for me. As much as it felt my life was over, little did I know how the baby would save me. She would force me to see the world in new ways and search for answers to questions I didn't know I even had. I returned to college and started finding answers. I still made bad choices in men, but I gave birth to two more beautiful children.

Though there was a burning desire for me to find the perfect mate, and try love again, it eluded me. I found mentors in school and work that led me to excel more and search more. It was my daughter's first pains of racism in school that led me to Ceremony. The bizarre part was that they were Cree ceremonies.

The movement of healing and empowering within the First Nations communities was just dawning. To white people, I was "Aboriginal," so that's what you do right? The perplexed look on their faces when I tried explaining, I'm Inuit, we don't do sweat lodge, was only met with confusion.

Then an Elder explained to me, "It's not about that, it's about building a sense of belonging." So, I went and was polite at first and got the concepts of prayer and agreed I would try. Who knew all the years of being forced to attend things would pay off in such a weird way?

At first, my First Nations friends thought I was odd but through Ceremony I listened and I learned. The manners I had learned years before had my kids and I cooking, sewing, dancing, and praying all over Alberta. At first, I didn't see the adults in Ceremony were on a path to living a clean life.

While I was busy for hours in the sweat lodge, my eldest began making friends with the children that grew up with their addict parents. With amazing speed, she learned that she could fit in, if she just joined in on the joints and stole smokes to share with these new friends. Soon came alcohol and a real quick jump to pills.

At fifteen years old, my daughter was in and out of my house, and getting arrested. She'd lost her virginity, gave her body up for drugs and dated boys that wanted to hit her. I was angry and frustrated, and the professionals did little to help. As they saw it, she had a good home, good parents, she was just going through a phase and would grow out of it. We were all wrong, very, very wrong. When she'd had enough at sixteen years old and wanted to clean up, she was too young to understand how withdrawal would help her get better.

She'd burned bridges and teachers didn't trust her. Her delinquencies gave adults reasons to criticize her and no assurance I offered her made her believe that this would pass. I began telling her how proud I was of her, and I took her to appointments. Three years of drugs and booze gave her eleven cavities and new eyeglasses. High school felt impossible to her because of all the times she had ditched junior high school. She would run away to her drug dealer, and I texted every hour, because I was sick with worry. I would ask her, "Are you ready? I'll pick you up, we'll figure it out together, come home, I love you, please, please."

Then the police came to tell me they had found her body the day before. Her shoplifting record allowed them to identify who she was by her fingerprints. She was gone. After a flurry of arrangements and dealing with family, I felt like I was walking through life like I was underwater.

I sat looking at her heartbroken ten-year-old sister and five-month-old brother and promised myself, they can't lose me too. No matter what. The lens in which I'd viewed the world was forever changed. I could never make decisions just to make people happy ever again, because it didn't matter to me anymore. It is true that there is no greater pain than losing a child, especially when you know they have taken their own life, that you couldn't make it better. I had to hold her sister after the police left and had no idea how I was going to put our broken hearts back together again. There is no sewing pattern or paragraph in shiny parenting magazines for this one.

At first I thought, I have Ceremony and the people that had become my family, but their pain was so great they couldn't look at us. We stopped being invited. Soon after my grandfather passed, my aunty lost a battle to cancer. My mother's residential school trauma never healed and soon alcohol took her liver and gave her cancer.

More young cousins left us through suicide. There's about five more years of *no air*. I didn't break completely, but I certainly cracked. I tried the glue called alcohol but that only made the world come apart more. I yelled at God, like an angered wife and turned my back on Him.

The funny thing is, the world keeps on turning, we search for sunny days and find time to lie on a beach. We run into friends and go for coffee and reconnect. When spring comes, we see the empty dirt in the garden and look for seedlings to fill it with flowers. A baby keeps growing, learning, and needing. None of it is perfect, because on planned days off, it rains or work keeps us from having time with friends, weeds keep trying to overpower the flowers and babies become moody teenagers. I have learned to live, accepting that there are many sides to every story and I am the editor. The ink may have dried on some chapters, but a good writer will review, edit and make changes.

It's been a tough journey I've set out on to date, but now I don't hold back for good or for bad. I have learned that there is no power in doing things to make others happy or worry about social standings or the like. There's been plenty of darkness that I have walked through. The darkness can feel like a miles-long forest fire with too much smoke leaving me unable to breathe. But my children remained my reserve oxygen, always with loving hugs to haul me out. Then, I finally gave myself permission to be happy,

I'm allowed to strive for happiness. There's no perfect solution and that's okay. I finally found a loving partner who added six more children of his own to our gypsy clan. I moved, got a new job with a non-profit where I'm with other Inuit and learning more of my culture every day. I'm trying to navigate a blended family and learning to pray again. The Creator doesn't give one or none of us fairness or justice; he is just able to love us no matter what. If we're able, we can accept this love, open it like the gift it is, and see it as a new day with endless options.

A STORY OF SHEER SURVIVAL

BY SHANE PEMENT

I am a survivor of the Sixties Scoop. I was born in 1968 in
Montreal, Quebec and taken only a couple of weeks later. I bounced
around from foster home to foster home, until I was two years
old. It was in October 1970 that a young couple came to the foster
home I was in, looking to adopt a boy. There were only two of us at
the time, me and a little Caucasian boy who was a little older. The
young couple thought it over and returned with me as their final
choice. The lady already had three girls and had lost two. The man
wanted a boy like most men do.

They were told they would have to visit me three to four times
before I could leave. Well, the second visit came around and the
lady from the foster home handed me to the young couple and
said, "You can take him today." The couple were not expecting this
sudden decision. I was wearing just a diaper; my new parents went
out and bought me some clothes and that was it. My father wanted
to give me a chance in life. He even fought for me, so I could have
my Native status.

After I was taken from the foster home, I was on my way
to Aylmer, Quebec. After a six hour drive, we finally arrived.
My father told me that I shook like a little puppy because I was
shivering so badly; I didn't say a word the whole ride home or at
any time during the next few weeks, for that matter. I was given

away so fast; the couple spoke to me in English only to find out later I only understood and spoke French.

As I stepped into my new home, three girls were standing at the front door, but there were no boys. I guess my mother could only give birth to girls, because she had another one six years later, so I was surrounded by girls.

I could understand why my father wanted a boy. But my mother was another story. I found out much later, around the age of eleven or twelve, that she didn't really want me—she had wanted the little Caucasian boy. But deep down, I don't think she liked boys. You will understand later.

My mother and I fought from day one. I'm not sure how I bad I was, but I know that it was a struggle for me. Maybe she didn't know how afraid I was. After three or four months, my mother would call the social worker over to try to settle me down, but everything just got worse. The relationship between my mother and I was very toxic. My mother would threaten me with, "Do you want to go back to where you came from?!" Who does that to a four- or five-year-old child?

I wanted to leave so much that they would tie my foot to the bed at night. During the day, I could remember being tied up in the back yard; the rope was just long enough to reach the little sand pit and I would play with my cars. Of course, my father worked all day back then, but I don't recall ever doing anything with my mother—colouring, or playing a game—I remember often hearing her tell me, "I don't have time."

I was always anxious for my dad to arrive, but that joy would soon disappear. Once he talked to Mom, I was cooked! The tears of the day would soon fill my eyes up again. I would soon realize that I would never be happy. I even left the house in the middle of the night and could be two to three blocks away. But the weekends were just incredible. I got to spend time with my dad, even if I always had to work every weekend. I didn't care, I was with my dad. Everything was forgotten for those two whole days that I could spend with him. Then Sunday night would arrive, and I would start worrying for the week to come. My mother and I were like fire and ice.

By the time I started school, life was a nightmare for me. The fighting between my mother and I was nonstop—we fought over everything I did. So, school just added to the fire. I lied a lot when

I was a kid, but it was impossible for me to have any freedom at home, and it stayed that way till I left home. My mother's sister would plead with my mother to let me go with her. She had four boys and I would be happier there. Even my grandmother would tell my mother the same.

Amazingly enough, I was at the top of my classes; I was smart in school and very bored. I was such a disturbance; the school would call three or four times a week. I liked school but I also liked being away from my mother. I realized I would not ever be able to please her. She criticized everything I did—it was never good enough. I could have a 92% on a report card and all I would hear was, "If you would study, you could do better." She was right but I was satisfied and did well. I gave myself a pat on the back and said to myself, "Good job." I would even get the occasional pat on the back from my teachers.

Our biggest fight was about my hair. When I saw my mother take out the scissors or clippers, I knew I was in for it. She would cut my hair exactly like they did to the boys in day schools—a brush cut. I would cry so hard, all I wanted was to have long hair, just like the Natives I saw on TV. So, every couple of months, it was a brush cut and a week or two in my room or the yard.

It was almost impossible to make friends. I couldn't do anything or go anywhere, and my mother never liked the boys that lived on my street—they were all bad. I just defied everything; my mom would tell me. She would say be in by 4:45 and I would arrive at 5:00 and would end up grounded for a week. I spent a lot of time alone. She would even give me lines to copy. I must have written thousands and thousands of words during the time I was there. I did not invite any of my friends over, for fear that she would humiliate me. I would tell her my friends didn't want to come here.

While we are on the topic of humiliation, one time she sat me at the kitchen table naked for lunch and supper because she felt I had my hand in my pants too often, which I think a lot of boys do around the ages of six to eight. Now, imagine there are four girls at the table. I cried throughout both meals and ate at the same time. After that, I began to really hate being in that house. I started having really bad nightmares, waking up drenched in sweat, screaming, No, No, No! Well, I'm fifty-two today and I still have those nightmares. Not as frequently, but I'm always running from something or someone. Still working on that today.

At this point, I didn't care anymore about what my mother wanted; I took the criticism and continued in my own way. Like I said, I was lost the day I stepped in that house. I remember high school was coming up and my mother thought a boarding school would straighten me out or even a private school. They were ready to pay a lot to get me away from the house, so I went along. The first private school was an all-boys high school and there was no way I was going to attend an all-boys school. So I failed the entry exam on purpose. The next school was in Rigaud, Quebec. It was a boarding school and that is where I wanted to go, so I passed with 86%—I would do anything to get out of the house. But unfortunately, I got sick three-quarters of the way through my first year, and my parents took me out to send me to regular high school in Aylmer. My life soon got even harder.

At this point, my mother was convinced I had started doing drugs while I was in boarding school. But no, I would start using mild drugs with my high school buddies in Aylmer. Drugs became my accomplice and soon I was selling to all my friends. My small circle of friends got bigger, and soon became a huge circle of friends who smoked what I brought to school. I had become what my parents didn't want me to become. I became ten times worse. I remember taking money from my mother's purse regularly so I could buy candy. More like breath mints to hide the weed smell that came from my mouth.

I needed a family to belong to, but not the one I was assigned to. I was so miserable because of one person, my mother! It was bad from day one. By the time I was fourteen years old, I was arrested for a break and entry, so I was sent to juvenile detention for about one year, then to a half-way house. I ran away to the Ontario side, Ottawa. I always thought I was wiser than the system. By 1986, I got caught in a police sting which earned me a cell in prison for eighteen months.

The funny thing about this was that one time my father—after one evening of physio, because I broke my leg—drove up to the front of the city prison and said, "If you don't change, this is where you will end up." Well, two weeks after I turned eighteen, it was exactly where I ended up.

I got deeper and deeper into the criminal world. But that's where I felt the most at home, and a part of a family. I had been gone for almost five years and never spoke to my adoptive parents.

I cut all ties with that family. I always thought my mom was trying to get me to leave, and she was successful.

It was after a long stay in prison—I got out roughly eighteen months later—that I went on a war path. I was climbing the ranks but by the time I was twenty-seven, I was waist deep in trouble. I was consuming so many drugs, it wasn't funny. I am six feet tall, and by the age of twenty-eight, I weighed in at 110 lbs. I was at the end of the road. It was either quit or somebody would find me dead. I had nothing left, not even a bag of clothes to my name. I had hit rock bottom.

I finally got up the nerves to call a rehabilitation centre in Hull, Quebec. I called from a phone booth and when they finally answered, I simply said I needed help. It had to be that night, or they would have picked me up dead somewhere. The guy who answered told me that it didn't work that way. I replied that it had to. Maybe he could hear it in my voice, it was probably the first time I hadn't lied in a long time. I sincerely wanted to stop using and drinking my life away. They sent me a cab and off I went to this detox centre. I had some very big issues that I had to deal with. I didn't even know who I was anymore.

I was given my own bedroom and had my first shower in a couple of weeks. I was at the point where I couldn't care less about what I was doing to myself. The first procedure consisted of one month of detox. This meant that I slept and ate and saw the doctors, who were there every day. I ended up receiving three months of detox. All I would do in my room was sleep and cry. I cried so much I had marks down each side of my cheeks, and somewhere during those three months, they had a doctor come in to remove my rigid contact lenses. They had stuck to my eyeballs because I hadn't removed them for at least a year. After this happened, one morning I woke up and realized I couldn't see anything. Everything was a blur, and it took me several minutes to realize I didn't have my contacts in. This made me not want to leave my room.

The doctor came in to see me and explained that I would have to spend at least six months without seeing well, and that my eyes were in bad shape. It was a couple of months later that I received glasses. I actually cried when I got them. To finally see faces! Although I was pretty good at putting voices with people.

I started being part of a new family. My mind was set on getting my life back. For me it was like taking baby steps, until even the trees, the grass, the sky looked completely different. It was like seeing for the first time. I even thought that the people around me smiled more and I was beginning to like the newer me.

My therapy was about four months, but somehow, I managed to stay for two to three months more. I was a basket case. My emotions were uncontrollable. It felt like I would never have control of myself and that it was so easy to step back into the world I knew best. So, I had seven months of being clean under my belt but that was nothing compared to what was waiting for me outside those walls. I felt safe with where I was. But I knew I had to face the music that was waiting for me. Everybody wanted a piece of me, pushers, the government, collection agencies.

In 1998, I was collecting welfare—a cheque of a little more than $500. There was no way I was going to be on welfare, so I found some work rebuilding chimneys. The money was actually not bad, but I wanted to aim much higher. So, I left the chimney job and started working for a guy who I met through Narcotics Anonymous. Actually, I met him at an NA camping event. He arrived in his boat on the beach and started to yell, "I hear there is a Native looking for some work."

I got up and went to introduce myself. I started working for him the following week. This man believed in me and I think that was all I needed to begin a new journey. He also paid for me to go to another retreat, so that I could reach even further into my soul and really clean out the skeletons in my closet. After those two weeks, I felt like I had removed a ton off my shoulders. I was ready to deal with my past.

I began paying my debts, which also included apologies where it was possible, I had pushers that had wiped my debt with them because they were proud that I was clean. Sounds funny to say but that's what it was. And there were others who would kick down my doors, put a pistol in my mouth and say it's time to pay. As you can see, I had to work very hard. I owed somewhere around sixty thousand dollars, and it took me three years to pay everybody back. It was nice having those debts paid back and to finally not have to look over my shoulder.

Once I was on the right track, I decided to start my own flooring company. I was very proud of myself but there were always obstacles that I had to surpass. One of the worst ones was when I had my hair down to my waist and people didn't like it. I felt like

I was judged quite a lot, and it made me feel uncomfortable because it made me feel like I wasn't being true to myself and who I was. I cut my hair off, but I felt like I was complying to what society wanted and it didn't go with how I felt.

During my time in therapy, I met a girl who became my girlfriend. We soon learned that it wasn't the right time, because we were both addicts. As addicts, everything is spur-of-the-moment; it is one of the traits of an addict, I discovered later on. Next thing you know, a couple of months pass, and I was on a trip crossing Canada by train. It was a gift to myself, for my first year of being clean.

While I was on this trip, my girlfriend called and told me she was pregnant. I was in no way ready for a child, I could barely keep it together. I finished my trip and after thinking about it, I decided to tell her I would stay present in the baby's life, even though we had broken up and she had decided to keep the baby.

We had joint custody and things were good for a couple of years but then things got bad again. I had finally learned how to deal with life without using, so I decided to go for custody of my son. I didn't like that every time I went to get my son, I had to change his clothes and wash him because he also smelled of cat urine, and his mom had been diagnosed with some health concerns. I had to fight for custody for two years, but finally won.

My son was now five and in good hands. I thank my son every day for being in my life. There is no better feeling than to wake up every morning with the sound of little feet coming into your room at 6:30 in the morning. It was way better than any drug I did. One morning though, I received a phone call from a police officer, and he told me that my son's mom had hung herself.

At first, I didn't want to believe it, but I had expected that type of call to come sooner or later. I wish it had never come. It took a whole week before I could tell my son. Every time I came to tell him, I would break down and cry, so I would turn away, so he didn't see me crying. It touched me more than I thought.

My life finally started to make sense and I was becoming more responsible. I continued to work for a couple of years but soon stopped because of knee problems. I decided to go back to school and took a computer course and graduated but I didn't continue in that field. I found it way too fast, and always changing.

I eventually went back to flooring for about two years, just before I met the most beautiful girl. She had really short hair with little barrettes and spoke so softly. I fell in love. One afternoon, it was pouring rain outside, and I stopped her as she was leaving the parking lot. I remember opening the passenger side door of my car and asking her if she would have lunch with me. After that initial meeting, we slowly we began to see each other. It was like being in high school all over again. I was in heaven. She was exactly what I needed at the time.

I was thirty-eight years old, and things were changing again. One year later my son and I moved in with her. She was twenty-one years old at the time and had just lost her parents. Despite the age gap, we completed each other. I thought I had finally met the right girl. I had so much energy; I guess I would say I was in my prime. In 2009, she announced she was pregnant. But this time I was ready for another baby, everything was perfect in my life. Or so I thought.

In 2008, I received a phone call from Child Welfare and before the woman on the phone could say anything I told her that everything was good with my oldest and I hung up the phone. A week later, she called again but this time she said this call was for me. So, I listened to what she had to say, and she announced that she had found my biological mother.

I think I almost passed out. I started shaking. So many questions were going through my head and I found myself asking myself, "What do I do?" I had been waiting all my life for this moment. I felt like a little kid, all excited to speak with her. The social worker said it would take another week or so to be able to talk with her. She had to verify if she was willing to talk with me. My birth mother agreed.

A week later, the call came in. I heard her voice for the first time, and I had spent a lifetime just imagining what she would be like, what she looked like. How she lived. We both were hesitant to speak and there were a lot of moments of silence. I was so nervous to speak. Our phone call didn't last long but she said she was coming to Gatineau, Quebec to see me. I couldn't even imagine! I was so nervous and afraid at the same time.

When she arrived in Gatineau, we went for supper. As I was entering the restaurant, I saw her sitting at a table. She was so beautiful. When our eyes met, I think we both melted into tears. As I approached her, she got up to greet me. We said, "Hello" and the hug I received from her was the hug I had been waiting for all my life. I could feel something between us. We sat down and started talking about everything. I would say that it was the best moment in my life.

That night, I didn't get any sleep. I knew I was going to see her the next morning to have breakfast and meet the rest of my little family, with my oldest son Jessey, and my girlfriend Kim who was pregnant with my second son. Christmas was around the corner and my mother surprised us with a pair of handmade gloves for each of us. They were beautiful. That morning was going way too fast. I didn't want it to finish and after finishing breakfast, they left to go back to Val d'Or. I think I drove my girlfriend crazy a little, because I could not stop talking about my mother! My girlfriend was very happy for me though.

Later, I found out I had three brothers. The oldest was a year younger than me. My mother sent me pictures of my brothers and herself when she was twenty-one years old. That was when she had me. I still wonder what it would have been like living with her and my brothers. I went up to Val d'Or the following year to meet my brothers. We had a blast telling stories to each other and I could see my mother watching us and laughing together. We went on like that for hours and she sat and watched us. I think she finally felt complete as a mother.

It was in 2010, while working one day, that I hurt my back. I took a couple of weeks off. It was in the second week that I woke up one morning and was in major pain on my left side. After a couple of days, I was almost in tears from the pain. I was rushed to the hospital and saw a doctor in the emergency. When they took an x-ray, they told me, "It's nothing to worry about, it will go away in a couple of weeks."

I headed home with a prescription of anti-inflammatory pills and a pain killer—a light morphine. But the pain went on for several months, and after a couple of visits to the emergency room all they did was send me back home with a much stronger dose of morphine.

By now I was a bit of a zombie, and my bed was now in the family room. I could barely move. I went back to emergency one last time by ambulance. As I was waiting to see the doctor, another doctor came to see how much pain I was in. I was lying there all crooked. She came over and asked me if she could lift my head up. As she starts to lift my head up, I could feel some relief.

I didn't want her to let go because I hadn't felt so relieved of the pain in four months. She made sure I was in the operating room the next morning at 7 AM. It turned out I had two vertebrae that were cracked in half, and they were damaging all my nerves that came out of the spinal cord. The damage was done, the risk of paralysis was very high because of where the pain was coming from. To this day I have problems with my arms and six months later I would find out that I had degenerative disc disease, with the pain now spreading to my legs.

This put a stop to a lot of things in my life. I wasn't able to pick up my son who at the time was eight months old, and that had me feeling heartbroken. I couldn't work and a lot of my hobbies had to stop also because I became very limited in what I could do. I also decided to leave my girlfriend of ten years and though making that decision was difficult, we still get along great, and she is happy today.

If I had my way, I would leave Gatineau and go live with my mother. I need to see her more. She is getting older, and I find it very hard. I'm alone today because of my health issues and I have an eleven-year-old boy that I cannot leave behind. My oldest is on his own and doing very well as an electrician. My kids are what have kept me going, like my mother's son kept her going. I think we both wanted the same thing.

STOLEN

BY ARLENE NOSKYE

My name is Arlene Noskye. It was in 1976, when I was four years old, that my four siblings and I were apprehended from our parents on Sturgeon Lake Cree Nation.

It was a warm summer day when my cousins were visiting at my Kokum's house, that my younger brother and I were playing when a van pulled into the yard, and my cousin told us, "Go, go hide in the bush."

My brother and I were living at my Kokum's and when we were told this, we hurriedly went down a path behind our Kokum's house, and crouched in the grass. I didn't answer anyone calling me but all of a sudden I heard my oldest sister yelling and calling my name.

I knew I had to go and see what she wanted. She had been coerced into calling me in order for me to come out of hiding. As soon as I came out of hiding, it was into the vehicle I went. My siblings and I were herded into the vehicle and away we went.

The first home we got taken to was on the reserve. It was horrible! We were made to eat on the floor. My brother and I were bedwetters and I assumed that was due to the trauma and abuse we suffered. When we wet our beds we were stripped naked and made to sleep on the floor with no blanket.

There are other memories that include my sister and I being locked in a dark closet for hours until the man wanted to have his way with us. It is hard to recall how long we were there. I just hope it wasn't too long. The next place I remember was the Grace

Children's Home. I only recall my one brother, sister and I being there. I believe my two youngest siblings were already on their way to their adoptive homes.

The building, Grace Children's Home, was a white two-storey brick house that looked almost jail-like. There were many kids there. They were of all ages and it included boys and girls. Again, while there I was punished for wetting the bed. My soiled sheets were held in my face. Molestation happened, not just with me. From the older kids too.

When we finally got to leave Grace Children's Home, my siblings and I were all separated. A farm way up North was one of the best places that I had been in thus far, even if I always felt out of place. At school I would get called squaw and they would yelp in the stereotypical Native war cry that mocked Natives.

I often dreaded when anything was taught about Indians. I was made to feel so ashamed. I recall many times where I soaked my hands in bleach and prayed that I would turn white. At my last home, I hid food the whole first year I was there and continued bed wetting. I was referred to as the "foster child" or "the girl." It wasn't until fourteen years later that I went back to my parents, but in my opinion I believed that it was a mistake. It was like culture shock.

My parents didn't know how to raise me, because all their kids had been taken away, and they had never been given a chance to raise us. I rebelled as much as I could. My mother and I rarely got along and I blamed her for our being taken. Though I blamed her, I'm glad that I did get to know my relatives again. I relearned a few Cree words, but sadly they didn't stay with me. My mom had told me before were taken, my siblings and I could all speak Cree, so essentially, I had lost my ability to speak my language fluently.

In becoming a parent myself, I have made many mistakes with my own children, but there was one thing I did and that was to always make sure that they would never ever be a part of the system.

The ordeal I went through was traumatic. I grappled with never feeling loved or feeling a sense of belonging. I despised the Native in me, felt tremendous hate for literally everyone and had no trust or faith in anyone or anything.

I pray for all survivors of the Sixties Scoop to continue to heal, to grow stronger and try and put this horrible experience to rest.

HOME AT LAST

BY ELIZABETH REDSKY

My name is Elizabeth Redsky and I am a fifty-six-year-old Ojibway woman, kookum (grandmother) mother, daughter, aunt, cousin and survivor of the Sixties Scoop.

I was adopted into an Irish immigrant family in 1963. My older sister used to tell me she picked me out of a room full of Ojibway babies. She picked me because I was crying my eyeballs out. I don't remember very much about my childhood. I've blanked it out. What I do remember from age four to age ten are sad times, being abandoned at family outings, being at summer camps I hated, being abused, being scared and intimidated by a big Indian man every time I walked to school. What helped me fall asleep at night was hearing a beat of a drum as I fell asleep.

When I think back to my childhood, I don't remember anything positive. I remember going shopping with my mom and other white mothers staring at us while we shopped. At first, I didn't really notice, but then I began to see that I had darker skin than my siblings. I had four white brothers and one white sister. The white mothers were staring at me because my skin was darker than my mom's. It was during that time that I didn't want to go shopping anymore, I didn't want to be stared at.

My brothers would tease me as well. They would tell me that I was a part of the family because my dad bought me for eight dollars. My brother who was the same age as me told me he was adopted into the family too. It was when I was around ten years old that I started to question, Why is my skin a different colour from my brothers and sister? And where am I really from? What does the word "adopted" mean? It was also the same time the beat of the drum became louder as I lay down to sleep.

My body was starting to change as well, I noticed my hips must've moved or something because now I could really wear jeans; they fit perfectly. For the next few years, I was thinking a lot about where I was from and who my mother was. These questions weren't very positive. I was dealing with abandonment, and wondering, "How could she?" and, "Who was she?" I was thirteen and the wondering was relentless.

My adoptive mom didn't have any information on my biological mom, but she did give me my adoption papers. My mother's signature was the only one on the adoption papers. I was experimenting with alcohol around this time and was already a seasoned pot smoker. I found a way to push away feelings and numb them.

My mom surprised me one day and asked me if I wanted to go meet my relatives in Shoal Lake, Ontario. I said yes. When making the arrangements, we called the Shoal Lake Band Office and learned the Redskys would be in Winnipeg, Manitoba, at a Powwow. So, it was agreed I would be leaving from Powell River to Winnipeg on an open return flight.

I was only thirteen years old and nervous and excited. As I laid down to sleep, once again I heard the beat of the drum loud and clear. Before I got on the plane to leave, my mom gave me cash and said, "When you get to Winnipeg, the first thing you should do is get a hotel room; not an expensive one either." So, in the nervous state I was in, I told the taxi driver I needed to get a cheap hotel. Omg! The hotel was really cheap, and I only remember the hotel across the street from mine was called the Occidental Hotel on Main Street in downtown Winnipeg.

I got to the Winnipeg Centre which was demolished years after, where the new MTS Centre was built. The Powwow was incredible. I was totally amazed at the beautiful dancers and the jingle dresses. As I stood there and saw the dancers and how their feet danced to the beat of the drum, I started to cry because the drumbeat I had been hearing through the years as I lay to sleep was the drumbeat calling me home.

I didn't know where to start when it came to trying to find my family because there were so many drums, and I didn't know the language. I came up to one drum and no one could understand me. This happened four or five times. But then I asked this one woman sitting at the drum if she knew Archie Redsky. She didn't understand me either, but she told me to ask this old man who was sitting at the drum. As I told him my name, he got up and came over to me. He hugged me tight, and said,

"You're home, you're finally home."

ABOUT THE AUTHORS

Anna Croxen is a retired grandmother of five children and eight beautiful grandchildren. She resides in Toronto, Ontario and enjoys spending a lot of crafting, healing, drumming, and singing with residential school and Sixties Scoop survivors. She enjoys every minute she spends with this group. She is also a traditional dancer and enjoys Powwows. In September 2022, she is getting married to a fantastic man that she loves deeply. She believes that life is beautiful and that she is very blessed.

Vonda J Knipfel lives and works in Regina, Saskatchewan. Her passion to help her community is what led her to where she is today. She enjoys many hobbies including biking, gardening, reading, fishing, and road trips. Her greatest treasures are her four grown children and thirteen little beings who call her "Grandma!" Vonda shares this life journey with her best friend and fellow scoop survivor Jay.

Shaun LaDue Born and raised in the Yukon, Shaun's lineage is Coastal Tlingit, Tagish, Kaska and Dena Tha'. He's part of the Crow Clan and a citizen of the Ross River Dena. Shaun has had a wide range of jobs and professions over the years, ranging from teacher, writer, and postal clerk. Currently he is a self-described Nomadic Handyman and Stitch Wizard. Shaun lives part time in the Yukon and travels Canada and the United States the rest of the year. He designs and builds camperized vehicles and tiny homes.

Alice McKay is an Anishinaabe/Cree woman, and a first-generation Sixties Scoop survivor, from Duck Bay and Fisher River Cree Nation. She was taken into the care of Child and Family Services (CFS) at just three weeks old. Following the brutal slaying of her father in a rooming house in Winnipeg's West Broadway neighbourhood in 1990, Alice was made a permanent ward in 1991. Despite the abuse she endured while in the care of numerous non-Indigenous foster homes and the trauma she still struggles to heal from, Alice became the first member of her immediate family to receive a post-secondary education after graduating from the University of Winnipeg with a degree in Education in 2021. She is currently teaching in Winnipeg, Manitoba.

D.B. McLeod is Ojibway from Sagamok Anishnawbek First Nation. A part of the last generation of the Sixties Scoop, D.B. was raised in the north west of Toronto by a non-Indigenous family. Denise proudly defines herself as an urban Indigenous Indigi-Queer woman, and is interested in the reclamation of language, culture and ceremony as that has been a large part of her healing. She began her career in frontline social service work in the United Kingdom working with people with intellectual disabilities. She has been an active member and works continuously in Toronto's urban Indigenous community. She dedicates her time and efforts to her passion: preserving the cultures and traditions of Indigenous/Anishinaabe peoples; she is committed to creating positive spaces that break down stereotypes and barriers where Indigenous peoples can be proud to identify their Nationhood. This especially flows through her work as a professor. She teaches Indigenous content at the post-secondary level.

D.B. is interested in the intersections of gender and sexuality, gender-based violence and Indigenous governance both professionally and through her own educational pursuits in the Urban Indigenous Education Graduate Program at York University. She is a very proud mother of two almost adult teenage(ish) humans, dog-mom to Etta, and a founding member of Toronto based Indigenous Women's comedy collective, Manifest Destiny's Child and Ode'Min Giizis Full Spectrum Doula Collective.

Christine Miskonoodinkwe Smith is a Saulteaux woman from Peguis First Nation and the author of *These Are the Stories: Memories of a 60s Scoop Survivor* published by Kegedonce Press in December 2021. She is an author, editor, writer, and journalist who graduated from the University of Toronto with a specialization in Aboriginal Studies in June 2011 and went on to receive her Master's in Education in Social Justice in June 2017. Her first non-fiction story "Choosing the Path to Healing" appeared in the 2006 anthology *Growing Up Girl: An Anthology of Voices from Marginalized Spaces*. She has written for the *Native Canadian, Anishinabek News, Windspeaker, FNH Magazine, New Tribe Magazine, Muskrat Magazine* and the *Piker Press*. She has also co-edited the anthology *Bawaajigan* with fellow Indigenous writer Nathan Niigan Noodin Adler.

David Mortimer was born Davy Turcotte in August 1967 in Winnipeg. He was taken into the foster care system at the age of one, where he was later moved to British Columbia without consent of his mother and adopted, with his identity changed to David Mortimer in January 1971. Today, David lives with his wife of over thirty years in Winnipeg. They are surrounded by a circle of many friends and family, where they raised their son, who is now a successful young adult. After a fifty-year search by his mother and birth family, David was reunited with his mother and five younger sisters in September 2019. They are finally back together as a family.

Arlene Noskye is a Cree woman from the Sturgeon Lake Cree Nation. She is a mother to three children. She has worked most of her life in the hospitality industry.

Karen Orser is an Inuit woman from Iqaluit, Nunavut. She is currently the manager of Employment and Training services and at Tungasuvvingat Inuit in Ottawa, Ontario. She returned to college as a mature student to do her Social Work diploma in 2000 and has worked predominantly in Indigenous non-profits over the last twenty-plus years since finishing. She considers herself a lifelong learner and is continuing her studies with Algonquin College currently doing an Applied Management Certificate. A self-proclaimed introvert, she found writing and sharing stories a good way to connect to her adopted family when she was too shy to talk to them face to face.

Doreen Parenteau is a Sixties Scoop Survivor, who is reconnecting and reclaiming her Indigenous identity and culture. She is originally from Treaty 4 territory and grew up and resides on Treaty 6 Territory. She has been a stay-at-home mom of three for the past nine years. She is due to graduate from the Community Support Diploma Program through Robertson College in the fall 2022. In her spare time Doreen enjoys walks and camping with her children and husband, volunteering with her children's various sports teams and creating and crafting. Writing has been an outlet on her healing journey and is helping Doreen find her voice. She hopes that by sharing her story she can inspire and help others find their voices.

Shane Pement is a fifty-four-year-old Algonquin from the Anishinaabe First Nations. Today, he is a full-time father of two magnificent boys. He is retired from the work force due to a degenerative disc disease. He has a great hobby—a little woodworking shop where he makes personalized cribbage boards and wooden puzzles. He describes himself as definitely being a fighter, and his best accomplishments are to have gotten clean at the age of twenty-eight, finding his mother at the age of thirty-eight, and finding himself while raising his boys. He is presently writing a book of his journey as a survivor.

Tyler Pennock, author of *Bones* (2020), is a Two-Spirit Queerdo from Faust, Alberta, and is a member of Sturgeon Lake Cree Nation. They were adopted from a Cree and Métis family and reunited with them in 2006. Tyler is a graduate of Guelph University's Creative Writing MFA program (2013), as well as the University of Toronto (2009). They have lived in Toronto for the past twenty-five years.

Cathy Phannenhour is an Indigenous Keynote Speaker. She aims to help individuals and organizations to expand their knowledge, connection and understanding of Indigenous issues. She has presented to both public and Catholic school boards, post-secondary institutes, hospitals and mental health organizations. She is an Ojibwe member of Big Grassy River First Nation, Treaty 3, in Northwestern Ontario. It is through her unique perspective as a Sixties Scoop survivor and her cultural storytelling that she challenges hidden bias and systemic beliefs while opening the door to new ways of thinking. She spent fifteen years working for the Department of National Defense as a civilian in the Logistics Branch, supporting troops and personnel at home and overseas. She is a lifelong learner studying Policing foundations, human resources, social service work, and continues Indigenous studies education. Since retirement Cathy has become a ReikI master and therapeutic touch and meditation practitioner. She hosts and attends weekly talking/sharing circles, learning language, culture, and ceremonies of the Anishinaabe. She continues to grow and thrive with the support of her husband, daughters, and family.

Elizabeth Redsky is a fifty-six-year-old Ojibway woman, kookum (grandmother) mother, daughter, aunt, cousin and a Survivor of the Sixties Scoop. It was when she returned to her home community to attend a Powwow that it was affirmed that she was "home at last."

Terry Swan is Cree/Saulteaux and a member of Cold Lake First Nations. Throughout her career she has been a passionate advocate for equality and social justice, and has led the development of nationally lauded prevention and healing programs to address ending violence against Indigenous women and girls. As sole proprietor of Wahkohtowin Consulting, she works as a traditional healer within community-based organizations. Terry is a lifelong writer whose work blends fiction, creative non-fiction, and poetry. She is currently writing her memoir, a story of her transformational healing journey as a Sixties Scoop survivor. She holds a M.Ed. from York University.

Melissa Thomas (Sigvaldason) lives in Winnipeg, Manitoba with her husband and two kids. She has earned four university degrees since 2009. Currently Melissa is a Kindergarten Teacher. She has a passion for incorporating Indigenous knowledge into the classroom. Her biggest career goal is to help all kids see their true potential.

Lisa Wilder was adopted at birth and raised in a Jewish family in Winnipeg, Manitoba. Unbeknownst to her parents, she had been placed in the adoption system without the consent or knowledge of her biological mother. As an adult, she connected with her biological family and learnt her truth—she and her older brother had been taken from their mother because she was a single Metis woman, during the time known as the Sixties Scoop. Having a foot in two different oppressed communities is what gives Lisa her drive to bring about change in this world, and she looks forward to continuing to carry on the traditions of her Jewish heritage, while proudly discovering and integrating those of her Indigenous roots as well. She now resides in Calgary, Alberta, where she is studying to become a counsellor, and is the proud mother of her two daughters, Megan and Mika, and step-son Matthew.

COVER ARTIST

George Littlechild was born in Alberta, the son of a Plains Cree mother and a Celtic father. A survivor of the Sixties Scoop, he was raised by foster parents in Edmonton. Littlechild received a diploma in art and design from Red Deer College in 1984, and a BFA from the Nova Scotia College of Art and Design, Halifax, in 1988. His mixed-media paintings are often socially charged in response to political movements, societal concerns such as reconciliation and reclamation, as well as personal history. He says of his work "I am committed to righting the wrongs that First Nations peoples have endured by creating art that focuses on cultural, social and political injustices. As an artist, educator and cultural worker, my goal is a better world. It is my job to show the pride, strength and beauty of First Nations people and cultures, and contribute to the betterment of mankind." George has exhibited in galleries around the world, and his art is in several important collections.